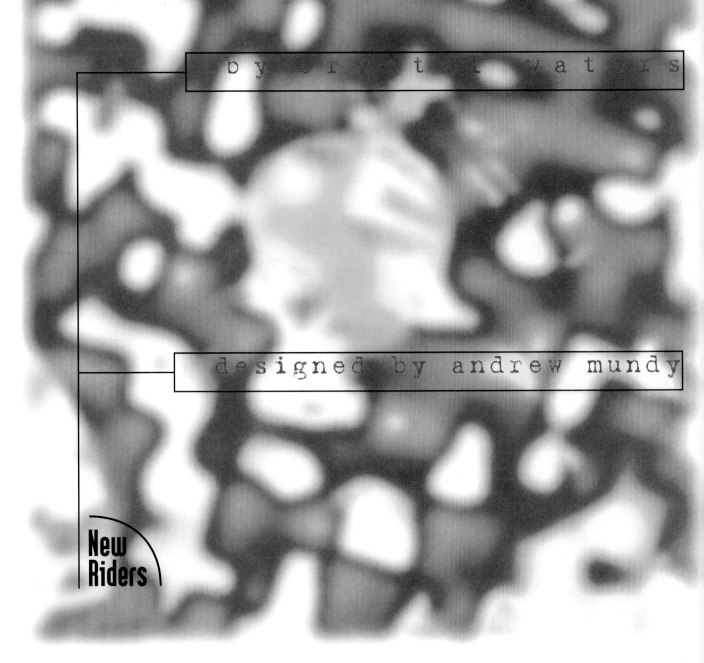

Web
concept & design

a comprehensive guide for creating effective web sites

by crystal waters

designed by andrew mundy

New
Riders

web concept & design

Crystal Waters

Published by:
New Riders Publishing
201 West 103rd Street
Indianapolis, IN 46290 USA

Printed in the United States of America   1 2 3 4 5 6 7 8 9

Library of Congress Cataloging–in–Publication Data

CIP data available upon request

This book was produced digitally by Macmillan Computer Publishing and manufactured using 100% computer-to-plate technology (filmless process), by Shepard Poorman Communications Corporation, Indianapolis, Indiana.

Warning and Disclaimer

Publisher	Don Fowley
Publishing Manager	Jim LeValley
Marketing Manager	Mary Foote
Managing Editor	Carla Hall

CREDITS

acquisitions

Jim LeValley

editor

Carla Hall

indexer

Sharon Hilgenberg

book design & layout

Andrew Mundy

associate product marketing manager

Tami Apple

new riders design team

Sandra Schroeder
Karen Ruggles

senior editor

Sarah Kearns

acquisitions coordinator

Tracy Turgeson

assistant to the publisher

Rosemary Lewis

editorial assistant

Karen Opal

e-mail us at: webmaster@mcp.com
jlevalley@newriders.mcp.com
chall@newriders.mcp.com

about the author

Crystal Waters (crystal@typo.com) writes about, creates, consults on, teaches about, reviews, and tests web sites and web technology. Formerly the features editor of *The Net*, she's done stints at *Computer Life* as online editor, ZiffNet/Mac as associate editor, *MacHome Journal* as senior editor, and *Home Office Computing* as west coast and reviews editor, and freelances for a number of magazines. Her web site, **typo.com** (http://www.typo.com), has received recognition as a Project Cool Sighting and as a Best of the Web site from c|net, among others.

about the designer

Andrew Mundy (ajmundy@cris.com), of Mundy Design Studios, is a San Francisco–based artist and designer who also teaches in the Multimedia Studies Program for San Francisco State University. His specialities include 2-D and 3-D animation and illustration. Visit his web site at http://www.cris.com/~ajmundy/.

trademark acknowledgments

All terms mentioned in this book that are known to be trademarks or service marks have been appropriately capitalized. New Riders Publishing cannot attest to the accuracy of this information. Use of a term in this book should not be regarded as affecting the validity of any trademark or service mark.

acknowlegments

"First things first, but not
necessarily in that order."

— Doctor Who

V

My first thanks and dedication go to my lovely little mom, **Leona Schultz Waters**, whose 73rd birthday happens to have coincided with the final deadline date for this book. While she says she doesn't understand a word I write, she still reads it all, and proudly shows it off to anyone who will look. I love you, Mom!

A very special thanks to **Andrew Mundy**, for endless encouragement, support, patience, love, companionship, and friendship—not to mention, some kick-ass design for this book. That's my story and I'm sticking to it.

Another special thanks to **Jim LeValley** and **Carla Hall**, my "team" at New Riders, for unending support and belief in this book. I don't think we ever spent more than five minutes of a two-hour conference call actually talking about the book, but we got it done anyway. Tattoo you, guys!

To **Lynda Weinman**, for everything, all the time—especially when it's three in the morning and we're on deadline, but we still manage to exchange an e-mail rant or ego boost before we collapse in exhaustion over our keyboards.

To **Jack Lyon**, senior editor at *PC/Computing* and one of my dearest friends, for encouragement, support, and tolerance of my occasional insanity.

To my sister **Lois Deberville**, who loves to live vicariously through me, and thanks to my other sister, **Diane Galway**, for not living vicariously through me. It all balances out in the end. Ernts to you both.

Internet the cat, for keeping my lap warm and for not accidentally erasing too much text when he decides to walk on the keyboard, which is like every five minutes.

To **Ben Templin**, for guidance and friendship and the cool jacket—and absolutely no legal advice.

ACKNOWLEDGMENTS

vi

Jeffy Milstead for friendship, answering my idiotic tech questions, and for making me laugh at silly jokes.

To **Nina Mullen** and **Joe Lambert** of the San Francisco Digital Media Center for pats on the back and letting me dance with their son **Massimo**.

And to so many other people: my fellow cynic and friend, **Lauren Guzak**; **Laurie McCullough**, for timeless friendship; **Sonia Plumb** of The Sonia Plumb Dance Company (my very first friend; we met when I was four and she was three) for following her dream and inspiring me to do the same; **Dan Thompson**, for always believing I could do this; **Kay Nelson** for unfailing trust and support of my work; **Kathy Tafel** for tolerating my rants and constant HTML questions when I first started getting obsessed with the stuff; **Jeff Dawson**, for inspiring hope and the urge to wear lipstick in public; **Dana Atchley** and **Denise Aungst** for encouraging me to tell my stories and shop at the Salvation Army for furniture; and **Bruce Heavin** for boosting my ego by trying to hack my web page counter. ;-)

Not to mention (but I will), **Shel Kimen** and **Minda Sandler** of *The Net*, **Deanna Vincent** of *Parent Soup*, **Nathan Shedroff** and **Drue Miller** of vivid, **Kat Flinn** of *Internet Underground*, **Nancy Eaton** of *RETRO*, **Teresa Campbell** of *MacUser*, **Ted Stevenson** of *Internet World*, the web folks at **Sirius** Communications, **Bryn** at Lyle Tuttle's, **Scott Rosenberg** of *Salon*, **Gandalf** (Andrew's cat), **Karen Wickre**, **Barbara Bergesen**, **Twescoo**, **Mark Frost**, **Chris Barr** of c|net, **Elise Bauer**, **Chris Charla**, **Jim Galbraith** of Spoto, **Coco Jones** of c|net, **McRoskey Airflex Mattress Company**, **Vince Broady** of GameSpot, **Jeff Gates** of In Our Path, and all the tolerant people who let me barrage them with questions about their web sites and web concept and design, especially those on the Web Design mailing list.

ACKNOWLEGMENTS

vii

A very special thank you goes to the **Havana Street** guys, A.J. Garces and Emery Wang, whose brilliant *In The Mood* fabulous 40's clipart graces the intro pages of each chapter, and can also be seen as spot art and examples throughout the book.

Havana Street can be reached at:
phone/orders—800 460 7624 or 512 479 1773
fax—512 892 5609
e-mail—havanaguys@aol.com
web site—http://www.eden.com/~havana
snail mail—7200 Chuck Wagon Trail, Austin, TX 78749

web concept & design

table of contents

TABLE OF CONTENTS

ix

TABLE OF CONTENTS

introduction
the phenomena of publishing on the web

"My mother overheard my father at
a cocktail party... someone asked
him what I was doing, and he
responded, 'Well, Margaret is working on the World Wide Web. I don't
really know what that is, but I
know it's very important.' I told
him that is the way most people in
the industry feel."

— Margaret Gould Stewart
Creative Director, Tripod Inc.
http://www.tripod.com/

Whatever statistics I could give you about the number of individuals and companies now publishing on the web, by the time this book got into your hands, that number would have grown tremendously. The thing about the web is that it affords the opportunity for anyone who has the equipment, the connection, and the where-with-all, to get stuff out there at a moment's notice. Anyone can publish, and they do.

Watch TV once in awhile, and you'll notice that nearly every show, every station, and sometimes every commercial has a web address. Radio shows not only have web sites, they're now broadcasting from the web. National chains, such as JC Penney and Ben & Jerry's, sport online stores and informational databases, and other vendors, such as book publishers and computer resellers, use the web as yet another way of not only doling out information, but actually selling products.

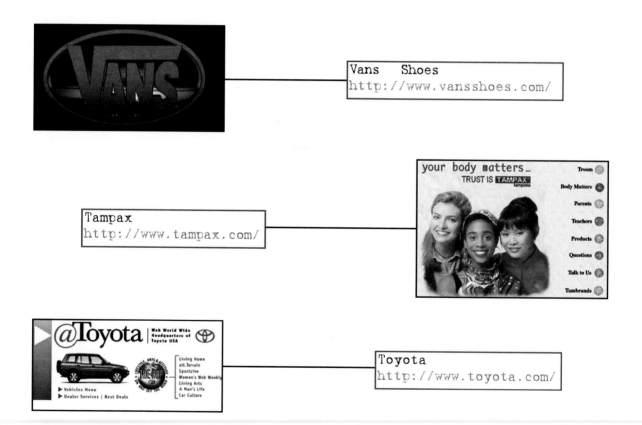

Vans Shoes
http://www.vansshoes.com/

Tampax
http://www.tampax.com/

Toyota
http://www.toyota.com/

NutraSweet
http://www.nutrasweet.com/

CompUSA
http://www.compusa/.com

Redbook
http://www.homearts.com/rb/
toc/00rbhpcl.htm

L.L.Bean
http://www.llbean.com/

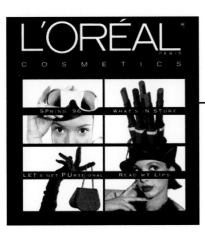

Loreal
http://www.loreal.com/

Campbell Soup Company
http://www.campbellsoups.com/

Ben & Jerry s Ice Cream
http://www.benjerry.com/

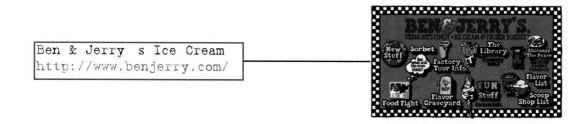

AMERICA'S ARMY

U.S. Army
http://www.army.mil/

Durex Condoms
http://www.durex.com/

Nabisco
http://www.nabisco.com/

And so, everyone wants a web site. And it seems like most everyone has one. It's cool. It's the whole "the future is here" race to the net.
Some are winning. A lot are losing, or at least wasting a whole
lot of time (theirs and ours). Some have jumped on it because they feel
they have to, and it shows. Some have taken advantage of the relative
ease the web affords to publish internationally. In what other medium
can an individual touting Zen legal advice and corporations as large as
Microsoft publish on a world-wide scale—and whose products, words,
thoughts, pictures, rants are accessible to whomever can get at them?
It's wondrous and frightening. The web is an almost instantaneous dis-
tribution method that churches, x-rated picture vendors, cat-food
makers, software companies, astrologers, the military, left-wing and
right-wing activists, artists, coffin constructors, and grocery stores tell
their stories, sell their products, and promote their wares.

```
1-800-Flowers
http://www.800flowers.com/
```

```
JC Penney
http://www.jcpenney.com/
```

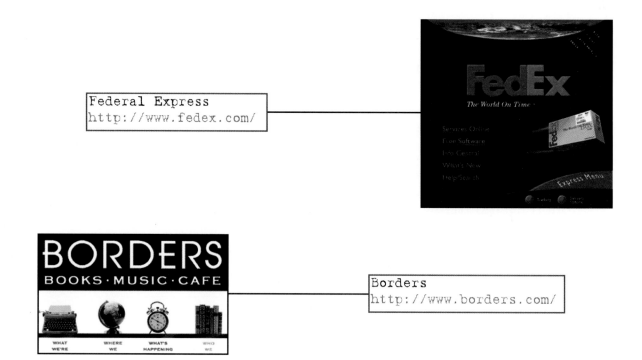

Federal Express
http://www.fedex.com/

Borders
http://www.borders.com/

Now that the major online services—i.e. America Online, CompuServe, and Prodigy—each give their combined 10 million–plus members free web space, that many more people now have at least two of the three elements of web publishing at hand (equipment and connection). These online companies, along with companies such as Adobe, also offer "instant" web-site-making software or online forms to get pages up fast. This is a good thing. But let's make it better.

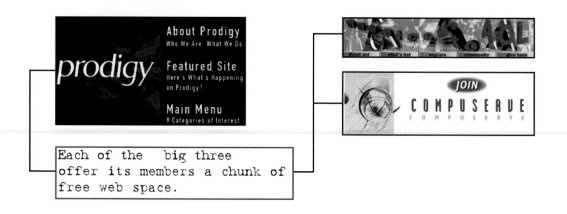

Each of the big three offer its members a chunk of free web space.

the design dilemma

The beauty of web publishing is that you can change almost anything at any time, hopefully to improve it. I'm one of those web people that constantly messes around with my site, trying to make it better; trying to hit on the perfect formula.

Why look for a formula? No one wants all web pages to look alike. But let's analogize for a second. Why do we still use the same basic gas-burning engines in our cars that were used in the original models almost a century ago? Because it works. And while designing for the web is much different than designing a car, good web design (like good car design) is based upon certain gut contents and concepts that keep them working, keep them moving, and get us where we want to go.

So whether you're the person in the company your boss has determined will be responsible for creating a web site, or you just want to promote your home business, put up a personal page with family photos, or one that delves into a particular obsession or hobby, you need to plan out what your formula will be. The key word in that last sentence is "planning." Your site doesn't have to look the same as everyone else's, but for it to succeed and bring people back, there are design guidelines that will help make the surf both more aesthetically pleasing and navigationally painless.

the web is more than HTML

Learning HTML code is obviously important—crucial—if one is to publish web pages. Either you or someone on your team should be proficient at coding. But it doesn't matter if you know all the codes well enough to recite them in your sleep, if you don't know what you want to do with them, you're left with a head full of tags and no where to go.

I teach web publishing classes at the San Francisco Digital Media Center. I tell my students right up front that we're going to spend some time planning what we want to code before I teach them any code at all. I show them sites that I think have good design, and sites that have bad design, and we discuss why each receive their given categorization. I then give the students an assignment to storyboard a site idea; sometimes it's a straight list of what they want to put on pages, and sometimes it's a collection of index cards to visually show the flow-through of the site. When it's time to go over the assignment, we brainstorm about improvements and throw around constructive criticisms of each other's sites.

But there's always the student who listens patiently through my demonstrations, the group's brainstorming, our talks about planning, planning, planning, and how we have to observe how people will use and navigate a site, and so on. "Yeah," the student says. "But when are we going to learn how to code? I want to learn to code NOW." These are generally the people who have looked in the classifieds and seen ads for $60,000-a-year webmasters, and have determined that they need only leave my class with <hr> and <align=right> and <bg color="#555555"> in their pockets, and easy street is theirs for the taking. Ain't so, bro. Great effects don't make a great movie (Johnny Neumonic, anyone?). I rest my case.

It's amazing to watch a student's face light up when a cohort remarks on, say, a restaurant site plan: "That's great... how about adding an area that explains which wine goes best with each meal you've suggested?" and it's something that they haven't thought of, and it's something that will help improve their site significantly. With this planning and constructive bantering behind them before students start to learn coding and how to prepare graphics for their web site, they have a visual and contextual goal in mind that helps connect the practical (the code) with the conceptual (the idea).

why this book exists

The reason this book was written was to help tackle the problems that so many sites have: lack of structure, purpose, unique value, navigational cues, and misplaced or misguided design elements. So many of the problems seen on web pages can be fixed or upgraded with just a bit of planning and forethought, and a few theories on how people use computers and view color and how iconic cues can help to make a site more than just a web-page-for-the-sake-of-a-web-page. This isn't an HTML book, it's a guide book meant to give you a hand through the planning, development, and creation of your web pages.

who this book is for

Web Concept & Design is written for both current and future web creators that may not have design backgrounds, or may have traditional design backgrounds and now want to apply that knowledge to the web. While we delve into many areas of web site construction and implementation, the goal of this book is to help teach you the basics of smart web page layout, design, and navigation, and show you why they work, no matter what the medium.

If you're a professional designer already, you'll be familiar with many of the theories outlined in this book. You'll also find that while the basic design rules are similar, the implementation is similar yet different for the web than, for example, print or CD-ROM-based multimedia.

If you're a coder, *Web Concept & Design* should serve to better your technique. You know what the codes can do, now let's make them do something that also looks good as well as takes advantage of every new whiz-bang standard that hits the books.

what's in this book (and how to use it)

Throughout *Web Concept & Design*, you'll find theories, visual examples, deconstructions, and instructions for making whatever site you work on work best for your viewers.

Wander through each chapter, or find the areas that you think you need to work on.

01. Evaluating Your Audience
Here's where you'll find out how to determine your site's goals and who you want to view and use it.

02. Brainstorming Content
You've got to fill a site with something, right? Here's some guidelines for getting the juices flowing.

03. Going With The Flow
How to flowchart content to determine initial site organization and planning site structure.

04. Page Elements
This chapter discusses page elements, such as font sizes, colors, and other visual cues used in traditional publishing that serve as navigational and identifying cues to site viewers.

05. Human-Computer Interfacing
You do realize that the web is used by "people," right? Looking through the basic theories and studies of human-computer interface design, we'll apply them to the web to increase usability, efficiency, and effectiveness.

06. Web Page Layout
Now we're ready to use traditional design concepts for web page layout and design, increasing navigability and visual appeal.

07. Storyboarding
Using this method of drawing out sample pages helps to visually place site elements and put page structure and flow into proper form.

08. Mood Lighting
Can the colors you choose for your web site make or break it? We look through some sites that use color effectively, to assist in picking the color scheme that best portrays your image.

09. Type & Style
Times Roman, Times Roman, Times Roman. This chapter explores the limitations and potentials of browser text, using type-treated images instead of browser-supported text, how to choose what type to use, and how best to present it.

10. Graphic Appeal
A picture can be worth a thousand words, as long as it doesn't take a thousand years to download. Here's some tips on using graphics as visual elements of pages; why and where they work and don't work, and web-specific requirements for graphics on pages.

INTRODUCTION

THE WEB

11

11. Gizmos, Gadgets, & GIF Animations

Is the whiz-bang worth the work? This chapter examines the impact and influences of new web technology, how it's been implemented, how it's used, when it is and is not appropriate.

12. Advertisements and Sponsorship

If you think you're going to sell space on your site, first see how others are doing it successfully. Chapter 13 discusses ad placement and size on a page, the separation of editorial vs. advertorial, and it takes a look at a variety of advertising models.

13. Interactivity

Want to keep in touch with your visitors? Here we'll tackle elements and technologies for encouraging viewer participation and feedback, such as mailto: tags and forms.

14. Viewing Choices

What looks good on your monitor may look bad on mine. Viewing Choices looks at advantages and disadvantages of designing for multiple browsers, and how to work around difficulties.

15. Testing, Testing

Think you're ready to announce your URL to the world? You better think again. Or at least go through this comprehensive checklist of crucial steps and tests before you go "live" with your site.

16. Web Designers Pet Peeves
    Web designers from a variety of sites
spout their views on what their biggest pet
peeves about the web and the evil elements
that make it up.

17. Outside Influences
    It ain't easy doing all this stuff your-
self. Just in case you're not a super-human,
I've included guidelines for hiring an outside
web design person or team to produce a site.
This section is helpful, too, for site designers as guidelines they can give to clients
about what they need.

the end is in (my) site

As with any publication made of this old fashioned paper stuff, we won't be able to fit everything in its pages, and new, important, crucial, damn–we–shoulda–put–that–in stuff will pop up the day the ink dries. So for updated information, additional links, and even some fun web toys and tricks, drop over to my site at http://www.typo.com/, or the *Web Concept & Design* site at New Riders (http://www.mcp/newriders/).

evaluating your audience

picking the people who view you

"I never design a building before I've seen the site and met the people who will be using it."

— Frank Lloyd Wright

15

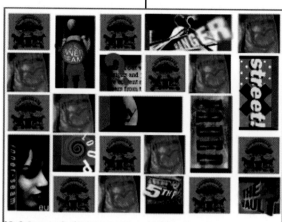

Like the jeans we make, this site is meant to be an original. It's a trip around many worlds, all on one globe. A trip that starts with you and never ends. Explore and enjoy.

HOME

Use the labeled graphics above to wander to the furthest reaches of our site. Or, scroll down and learn what's new before you take the leap.

Fly Zone
RAVE

Zone in on who and what's got it going on around the world. Now appearing, sick RAVE-ing mad DJs.

US: Inner Seam
ANIMATION

Step behind the scenes of three award-winning animated commercials from Levi's® Jeans for Women in the U.S.

EU: Inner Seam
WASHROOM

Take an exciting look at the latest TV spot for Levi's® 501® Jeans in Europe. Denim never looked so dangerous.

We welcome a new kind of interactivity with Levi's® Magic Painting, our first brush with Shockwave.

Faded
1930s

Come aboard the Levi's® time machine for a quick blast into the past. It's test time in Faded. You do remember the 1930s, don't you?

Street
TOKYO

It's fashion at street level. Get a grip on the youth tribes of Yoyogi Park. Formation dancing is only one step to Tokyo's stylistic conclusion.

Hanger
WAIST, INSEAM, ETC.

Where else would we keep our famous Levi's® Jeans but in the biggest closet on the Web?

Loop
WILD SITES

Swing by and check out our latest hot links to other wild and worthy sites. And don't forget to find your way back.

Fifth Pocket
NEW PRIZE

How about some fun and games? Now you can win a copy of one of the most mysterious Levi's® commercials ever made.

THE VAULT

In here is where we store everything that's ever been on this site. But the vault isn't locked. Come see what you might have missed.

HELP

If you need some, here's where you find it.

Questions? Comments? Tell us what you think!

It's not hard to figure out who Levis is targeting with its site: people with active lifestyles, both men and women, teens through X-gen, people using Netscape or other browsers that support its animation, people who are into "cool" things, including contests and rad links, and who have the time and bandwidth to spend looking through its site.

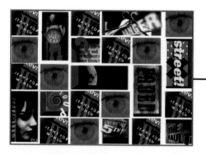

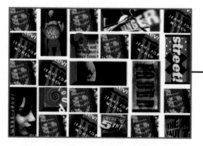

Trying to figure out what's left that's good to put on a web site can be mind-throbbing. Anyone who's spent any time on the web at all knows that there's a lot of junk in all that cyberspace, and you certainly don't want to be junk—at least, that's an assumption I'm going to take the luxury of making.

The web is also home to tons of cool art, writings, resources, and a sprinkling of animated GIFs and random-link generators that are actually worth looking at if you're willing to find them. There's a myriad of thoughts, pictures, products, and people, as well as home pages that have priceless content and wit, eye-tantalizing graphics, web concept and design trickery, and educational and entertainment resources that have become tremendously popular and successful.

So, how do you compete?

Before we answer that question, we have to determine just who it is that you are competing for. In the process, we've also got to ask "what makes a good site?" Some would say lively artwork, cool background tiles, or any new JavaScript or other plug-in. Beautiful graphics are one thing—but what if you went to a site to find out about a product, and the only thing you're met with is psychedelic animations and a Java script that crashes your machine?

There are times we want to spend time and money at our favorite French restaurant because the food is great, the atmosphere is cozy, the waitrons are exceptional and attentive, and the music is soothing. Other times we have 16 seconds and 99 cents for lunch, and drive-thru Taco Bell service is all we can deal with. Both "food access" methods survive, because both are wanted by a particular audience, at a particular time, place, mood, what-have-you.

The best sites are those that serve their audience well. From sites that give up-to-the-minute weather and road conditions in Lake Tahoe in text format (for those on their way out the door; who don't have much time; who need to know just what to expect on the way to their destination), to those that tantalize you with quizzes and mysteries and contests and wacky graphical characters (for those who have some spare time to seek entertainment or challenges)—if it gives you what you want without extraneous complications in the time frame you have available to spend, then a site is successful.

CHAPTER 1 YOUR AUDIENCE

17

TIP: PLANNING

Do you really need to go through all this trouble if you just want to put up a web page showing off photographs of your sneaker collection? Well, try giving some thought to why you want to go to the trouble of scanning and posting your footwear, or the potential for your creative work. Perhaps it could lead to being the foremost authority on used tennis shoes. Maybe you could get big advertising bucks from Nike...

first step: determining your site's goal

Before you fill your head with virtual sugar plums, plans of the little search engines that could, and how you're going to be Cool Site of the Day for eight days in a row because your graphics are as amazing as the sunrise (not that I think you're that grandiose), let's actually do some ground-floor planning. It's time to ask yourself: "What result do I want from creating my web site?"

There are a number of reasons to create a web site. Look through this list, grab a piece of paper or a stack of index cards, and make a list of your own. Feel free to add reasons if you come up with more. Pick as many as you like for now. Some topics may sound a bit silly, weird, or irrelevant, but no one else need see your list but you. We'll worry later about organizing the list of ideas or whether or not they can actually be implemented.

There's no need to get too specific about topics. Right now we're just trying to brainstorm a bit.

Ready? Recite after me:

"I want to create a site in order to..."

promote a product

promote a service

sell products

sell a service

sell advertising space

raise money/donations

tell customers about my company

enhance my company's image

change my company's image

create a community

tell a story

receive feedback from customers

post calendars or schedules

show off my HTML skills

show off my web design skills

learn HTML skills

fulfill a class assignment

complete a work assignment

promote my resume

promote my writing/portfolio

teach people a skill

create an alternate way for people to learn about me

create an alternate way for people to learn about my company

give employees internal information

post job opportunities

give product support (i.e., FAQs about products)

entertain my audience

research a subject

publish views on a subject

receive e-mail from potential penpals

support an existing publication,

support an organization, store, TV show, and so on

provide complementary information to other media

provide shareware or demos of products

provide a unique resource on a topic

push technology's envelope (i.e., experimentation with web technologies such as VRML and Java)

enter the 20th century (i.e., I need/ my company needs a web page because everyone else has one)

meet people

get rich

get famous

second step: who needs it? who wants it?

Now that we have a general idea of what we want to get out there, just who is it that we want to view the thing? For example, if you're creating a site with the goal to promote your graphic design/illustration skills and get freelance gigs, just who do you want to come see your work? Here's a sample list:

> your friends
>
> galleries
>
> book publishers
>
> magazine editors
>
> your parents
>
> art directors
>
> advertising firms
>
> web designers
>
> people who do the hiring
>
> companies with big budgets
>
> people with fast access to the web so that images load faster
>
> people with high-res monitors (able to view over 256 colors)
>
> people who use the latest browser versions (for special effects)

In your case, the age and sex of the audience is irrelevant, unless you have a very particular style or prefer to work for certain organizations or genre of publication, such as senior citizen gardening guides or children's comic books.

But if your goal is to support an existing publication about electric guitars, for example, your target audience may have some or all of the following characteristics:

> goes to concerts
>
> buys lots of CDs

collects guitars

has an interest in guitars

plays the guitar

may want to subscribe

loves Jimi Hendrix

is age 12 to 50 with a median age of 19

is more likely male than female

is part of a band

wants to be in a band

still has a day job (not a high tax–bracketed one)

monitor only supports 256 colors

28.8 or slower dial–in access

accesses the web via online services (AOL/CompuServe/Prodigy)

So let's get out another index card or two, and make another list profiling the people you want to bring to your site. Even if you think a category is irrelevant, try filling it anyway: you might trip over something good. If you've done market research or surveys already, now's the time to break out the data. But remember, we want to write down **who we want to bring to the site**, not just people we think may be slightly interested.

age range

sex

sexual orientation

marital status

family status (do they have children? how many?)

ethnic group

religion or lack thereof

political affiliation

salary level

budget/spending level

level of education (high school, college, doctorate)

type of education (medical, technical, artistic)

level of computer experience

level of Internet experience

type of job experience

type/speed of connection (i.e., T1, ISDN, 28.8 modem, 14.4 modem)

accesses the web from home

accesses the web from work

current job

amount of time they spend online

time of day/night they access the web

type of computer (low end, high end)

type of monitor resolution (256 colors; millions of colors)

computer platform (Windows, Macintosh, Amiga, Newton)

what browser they use to access the web (Netscape Navigator? AOL?)

hobbies

interests

pastimes

organizations they belong to

publications they read

television shows they watch

music they listen to

movies they see

food they eat (gourmet? budget? vegetarian?)

restaurants they frequent

country in which they live

area of the country in which they live

type of clothing they wear

credit standing

preferred way of shopping (mail order? shopping malls?)

level of spending control (i.e., buyer of goods and services for a large corporation or teenager with an allowance)

type of living environment (country, city, suburb, apartment, house, condo)

whether or not they have to call long-distance to access the web (no local dial-in numbers)

Again, there's probably a few profile categories that you'll come up with that I missed. Write those on your list.

where do you find marketing information?

If you don't have ready access to a set of marketing survey results, then take a look at some sites that provide results from basic consumer online information surveys.

For example, the GVU WWW User Survey Home Page (The Georgia Institute for Technology's Graphic, Visualization, & Usability Center's World Wide Web User Survey—http://www.cc.gatech.edu/gvu/user_surveys/) is endorsed by the World Wide Web Consortium (W3C), the NCSA's Software Development Group (SDG) (the Mosaic developers), and INRIA (the acting European host for the W3C in collaboration with CERN). According to its site info, over 23,000 unique responses were collected, and the results cover such categories as general demographics, browser usage, consumer attitudes, and preferences.

step 3: what do you do with all this stuff?

Ah ha, the clincher. After you determine a general description of the type of person who you'd like to visit your site, you can then use the information to help determine a number of design aspects for your site. Let's take a look at some of the user attributes, and show what those attributes can mean to your design.

Age range: could determine color scheme (bright crazy colors for kids; larger text for older viewers); language usage (some may not be legal or preferable for a younger audience).

Family status: could determine how much time they spend on the web. Kids could use it to study, but family may also spend more time doing things other than browse the web during the summer.

Budget/Spending level: may determine amount of time spent on the web (most people have to pay for access, some hourly); will definitely determine how much they buy (if you're trying to sell products).

Level of computer experience: heavily influences how much the viewer needs to be guided through different activities on a site (how to download a file; how to add a plug-in or helper application).

Accesses the web from home/Accesses the web from work/Whether or not they have to call long-distance to access the web (no local dial-in numbers)/Type/Speed of connection (i.e., T1, ISDN, 28.8 modem, 14.4 modem): all of these will help determine just how much time people have to spend on the web (if at work or slow connection, either a boss may be looking over their shoulder or they have to spend more time/money accessing). Will help determine if large graphics can be tolerable; will help determine length of pages.

Type of monitor resolution/Computer platform/What browser: each of these will influence what resolution graphics are preferable; what tags will be best avoided or taken advantage of (there's no use in creating Shockwave files if most of your viewers can't use them).

Hobbies/Interests/Pastimes: if your site isn't a hobbies/interest/pastime of your viewers, it may at least be able to include links (or perhaps a searchable database) to various sites or other resources of interest within the hobbies/interests/pastimes they enjoy.

Country in which they live/Area of the country in which they live: could determine what content is legally presentable or what software can be posted for download. If you're planning to sell products over the web, these factors will also determine what kind of tax, shipping costs, shipping limitations, and other information must be provided.

Preferred way of shopping: will help to assess whether you should provide an area for online ordering (if your viewers are used to shopping via credit card and mail order, they probably will be more comfortable shopping through the web), and help to determine what level of security you will offer customers.

summary

Before you can delve into the design of your site, you've got to determine **what** you want it to portray, **who** you want to view and use it, and **how** they will use it. If you want to promote your line of hand–woven designer silk scarves and sell them through your site, your audience will be different than that of a site dedicated to promoting the use of Rolaids as Barbie hockey pucks, a site that is a family history photo album, or an ice cream company's internal site explaining employee benefit information.

Once we do start getting into the actual structural planning for your site, this "image" that all this information helped create will help to determine such things as the kinds of graphics, the color combinations and contrasts of type and backgrounds, what sorts of interactive features you'll need, and even what browser to create for. This foundational research and brainstorming helps to solidify the goal and carry off the plan.

brainstorming content
the stuff your site is made of

"Daring ideas are like chessmen
moved forward. They may be beaten,
but they may start a winning game."

—Goethe

All this time you thought content was king, right? Until you spent an hour or two (hopefully) making the two lists in the previous chapter.

Now we're finally going to do some brainstorming about what's actually going into the site—then we'll start dealing with how it's organized. The actual structure comes a little way down the line.

Time to get out lots of index cards, because rather than a list, we're going to put each topic we come up with on the top of each card.

TIP: STUPID IDEAS

To properly brainstorm, you've got to let go of thinking that an idea may be silly or stupid or impossible. Write them all down, no matter what they are. You'd be amazed at some of the things you come up with, and what cool things may come out of them.

first step: determining your site's goal

The example I'll use is Bonnie's Bed & Breakfast, a fictional seven room Victorian in a small town in the Gold Country, near the California Sierra Nevada mountains. Note that my brainstorm list is in no particular order, nor is there any attention paid to just how realistic a category can be carried out. This is just idea time. When you're brainstorming, think of **EVERY**thing that may be unique about what your subject matter is.

Bonnie's Bed & Breakfast content list

where we're located
room rates
pictures of each room
pictures of the building
history of the building
history of Victorian houses
the remodeling after purchase
history of town
history of area
map of town
proximity to other scenic areas
directions to BB&B by car
directions to BB&B by bus
directions to BB&B by plane
car rental agencies
phone number
times of year we're open
menus
recipes
souvenirs
special seasonal deals
honeymoon suite
nearby activities
nearby restaurants
nearby bars
group rates
party planning
catering
reservation requirements
payment methods
staff profiles
the famous BB&B "ghost"
claw foot bathtubs
sauna
parking
famous guests
guest comments & complements
FAQs about BB&B

pet policy
children policy
daycare
weather
what to wear
what to pack
hiking routes
high-altitude precautions
breakfast schedule
gourmet coffee
special diet/menu requests
nearby health facilities
work-out room
biking
room themes
beds
phones
rating
organizations we belong to
what the press has said about us
antiques
quilts
seasonal fairs and events
panning for gold
guided tours
job opportunities at BB&B
emergency phone numbers
other web sites of interest
gift certificates
discounts at local eateries
local plant life
local wildlife
rules about camping
forest fire hazards
deposit policy
check policy
how to make a reservation

organizing content: the start of site structure

Ready for a hard part? It's time to sort the index cards into related categories. Don't worry about the actual final names for the categories at this point, they'll fall into place as you start sorting. Feel free to copy a card and put it into more than one category. This is actually a lot easier than putting up a site and having to rearrange everything after the fact, trust me. . .

Clear some floor or table space, or get some tacks and a big bulletin board or wall, and start putting out the cards. For example, as I lay out the cards for BB&B, I found that certain categories emerged. See how they fall:

About BB&B

menus

pictures of each room

pictures of the building*

where we're located

phone number

times of year we're open

staff profiles

the famous BB&B "ghost"*

guest comments & complements

FAQs (frequently asked questions) about BB&B

breakfast schedule

room themes*

rating

organizations we belong to

what the press has said about us

job opportunities at BB&B

*indicates items appearing in more than one category.

The History of BB&B

history of building

pictures of the building*

history of Victorian houses

the remodeling after we bought it

history of town

history of area

map of town*

the famous BB&B "ghost"*

famous people who have stayed here

antiques*

quilts*

About the Area

special seasonal deals*

map of town*

proximity to other scenic areas

nearby activities

nearby restaurants

nearby bars

weather

hiking routes

high-altitude precautions

nearby health facilities

biking

seasonal fairs and events

31

panning for gold

guided tours

emergency phone numbers

other web sites of interest*

discounts for guests at local eateries

local plant and wildlife

Planning Your Trip

directions to BB&B by car

directions to BB&B by bus

directions to BB&B by plane

how to make a reservation

car rental agencies

what to wear

what to pack

other web sites of interest*

deposit policy*

how to make a reservation*

Unique BB&B Features & Services

recipes

souvenirs

party planning

catering

honeymoon suite

claw foot bathtubs

sauna

parking

daycare

gourmet coffee

menu requests (vegetarian, dairy free, etc.)

work-out room

room themes*

beds

phones

antiques*

quilts*

gift certificates*

guest referral discount

BB&B Policies & Rates

room rates

special seasonal deals*

check policy

group rates

reservation requirements

payment methods

pet policy

children policy

gift certificates*

deposit policy*

check policy

how to make a reservation*

You may have just felt like you were playing with a very complex jigsaw puzzle, and in effect, you were—a three-dimensional one.

CHAPTER 2

CONTENT

33

but... what if my site is different?

While your content may be radically different than that of one proposed for a bed and breakfast site, this hands–on practice can be applied to any site planning process. This kind of paper puzzle is a necessary step in the organization of your site's content, no matter what it may be, and will be crucial to future design of the site.

TIP: PAPER SUCKS

If the thought of sticking index cards to your floor or wall just doesn't cut it, try out a piece of software to tackle the task.

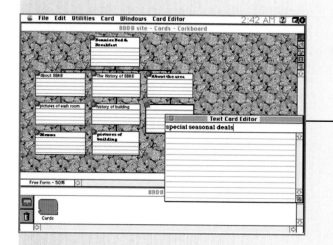

For the Mac:
three by five from
MacToolKit (pictured);
1234 6th Street 204,
Santa Monica, CA 90401;
800.231.4055,
210.395.4242.

Look familiar? three by five is a very intuitive program that works just like the paper does, only a bit smaller and easier to organize.

sorting: more ways than one

You'll probably find that there are numerous ways to sort your site's content. That's fine, and expected. As long as you keep to specific, well-defined (yet general) categories with logical subcategories, you should be able to hit upon a combination that not only works for you in the implementation of the site, but especially for your visitors when they start hanging out there. In any case, remember that it's easier to rearrange your entire site contents at this stage (and on paper) than after you get your site started or before you attack an entire site redesign.

summary

You've probably found that there's a lot more to the potential content of your site if you throw your limits down. If you're comfortable with it, bring in others to help you brainstorm ideas for content. At this point in the game, you haven't made any promises to your clients, only explored the reaches of what your site could become.

All the information in the world doesn't come in handy if there's no way of finding it. Taking some time to play your index cards not only helps you to begin the organization of your site's content, but also helps to start breaking it down into workable, real-life chunks that you can work on one at a time.

going with the flow
charting content & workflow

"Transforming data into information
is done by organizing it into a
meaningful form, presenting it in
meaningful and appropriate ways,
and communicating the context
around it."

—Nathan Shedroff, creative director, vivid

37

If you've gotten your list together of all the stuff you want to put on your site, and spread all your index cards all over the floor in a few relatively relative piles, you're ready to move on to the next step.

This is what the folks call flow-charting—and it works in the same way that a company's organizational chart does. Usually starting from the top (the president or CEO of a company), the branches flow down (five vice presidents, 10 semi-vice presidents or department heads each below each of them), all the way down to junior janitor.

While something may be "lower down" on your site, it doesn't mean that it ranks any "lower" than the rest of the content. Plus, all we're really doing is organizing ideas for content, not settling on the exact structure of the site.

TIP: MAPPING

While some pages tout many more choices than six on the first level, I recommend that you try to break down your topics into five to ten categories max.

You can always include a site map, which lists all content on your site. Can you see how your flow chart could easily translate into a site map, like the ones shown here from clnet and Adobe?

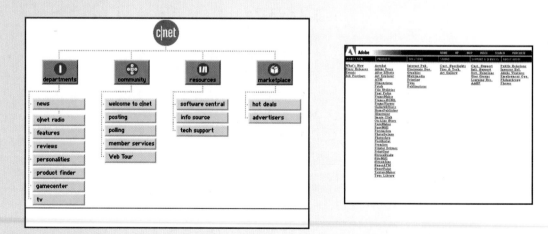

You can find these maps at http://www.cnet.com/Map/ and http://www.adobe.com/misc/sitemap.html, respectively.

Let's keep going with Bonnie's Bed & Breakfast. So far, we split up the index cards into six categories:

1. About BB&B
2. The History of BB&B
3. About the Area
4. Planning Your Trip
5. Unique BB&B Features & Services
6. BB&B Policies & Rates

Here's an example of how one of the Bonnie's Bed & Breakfast categories could break down:

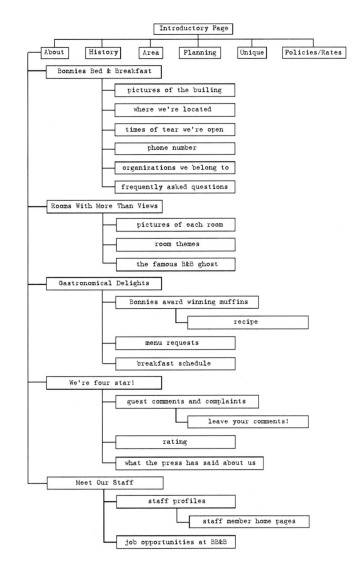

We're beginning to see how Bonnie's Bed & Breakfast site is falling into place. The entire process can take a while, but the beauty here is that you can move things around and start to conceptualize the organizational context of your content—a rough map of your overall layout. If it starts to make sense at this point, it will only make it easier as you actually start putting pages up on the web.

I hope too that it's easy to see why sites that start by putting up as much information as possible just to get up there can experience backlash when trying to link everything up.

the blueprints

Structuring your site in a flow chart not only helps to give you the visual and navigational feel of a site, it's also a great way to help you organize the actual construction of a site. A project this big with this much information is a daunting task—and there are many sites out there with even more information to throw around and organize.

In Anne Lamott's sublime book on writing, *Bird by Bird*, she tells a story about how her brother was intimidated by a school project:

> Thirty years ago my older brother, who was ten years old at the time, was trying to get a report on birds written that he'd had three months to write. [It] was due the next day. We were out at our family cabin in Bolinas, and he was at the kitchen table close to tears, surrounded by binder paper and pencils and unopened books on birds, immobilized by the hugeness of the task ahead. Then my father sat down beside him, put his arm around my brother's shoulder, and said, "Bird by bird, buddy. Just take it bird by bird."[1]

I guess I'd paraphrase by saying, "URL by URL, buddy. Just take it URL by URL." Even if your site is due tomorrow (which I sincerely hope is not true), taking it a step at a time is a lot less disheartening, especially if you're the lone webmeister.

With an outline/site map in hand, we're able to break down a project by page, by area, or by task.

[1] *Bird by Bird*, Some Instructions on Writing and Life, by Anne Lamott. 1994, Pantheon Books, ISBN 0-679-43520-4. Also check out the Anne Lammott site at http://www.typo.com/lamott/lamott.html.

Once you've decided on what tasks you'll pursue yourself, or decided on the order in which you've decided to do them, you're ready to move on to working on the actual physical presentation of the site. See pages 43–45 for some example work flow outlines for the construction of a web site story or section.

TIP: GOING OUTSIDE

If you're not sure what tasks you'll do yourself, or whether or not you decide to take on your web construction in-house or think you might like to hire an independent firm or contractor, read through the chapter on Outside Influences: Guidelines for Hiring Independent Web Site Designers (page 255). By familiarizing yourself with what outside designers expect of you, you'll be able to more easily understand what you or your company's people may realistically be able to take on.

the foundation is in site

Keep in mind we're talking structural presentation, not visual presentation when you're working on charting your site at this point. Before we can design a page visually, it has to be determined what each page needs as far as user interaction and informational needs of your viewers.

Let's take one part of the *About* section in Bonnie's Bed & Breakfast (see page 30) and analyze its content to determine what elements need to be considered before tackling the layout. The goal of this exercise is to create a plan that will enhance the efficiency (such as how easy it is to update), usefulness, and navigational usability of the site. We'll also take note of any logical relationships of this page to the others on the site or on other people's web pages.

Bonnie's Bed & Breakfast

   photos of the building*

   where we're located

   times of year we're open

   phone number

   organizations we belong to

   frequently asked questions about BB&B

Optional elements of this area, with notes on links and elements that can be easily changed or updated:

- photographs of the outside of the building (captions under each photo)
  - photos can change seasonally
  - link "click here to see the building in 'spring' 'summer' 'fall' winter'"
  - link "click here to find out about the history of BB&B"
  - link to "photos of each room"
- where we're located
  - text directions
  - view a GIF of a map
  - download a GIF of a map
  - link to "area" section
- times of year we're open
  - text with dates
- updateable calendar that shows when rooms are available (updated weekly)
  - links to different months of the year
  - form to send for availability of rooms
  - link to "seasonal deals"
  - link to "seasonal events"
  - maybe sell ad space to local vendors
- phone number
  - other contact information
  - e-mail address with link
- organizations we belong to
  - links to organizations that have pages
  - if no pages, create explanation of organization and provide information where potential visitors can write or call to find out about us
- frequently asked questions about BB&B
  - include form or mail-to for submission of questions
  - link to "we're four star"

* indicates items appearing in more than one category.

work flow basics

While there's no set way that a site's workflow should be set up, there's a lot to be learned from traditional editorial workflow that is applicable to putting together the work-flow process for a web site, especially if it's to be a site that is regularly updated.

members of print team: freelance writers, freelance artists, editor(s), copy editor(s), art director, art/production department, service bureau/printer.

article is conceived by editorial team

article assigned to writer by editor

writer writes article

writer turns in article to editor

editor reads article and edits it

editor discusses article with art director

editor turns article over to copy editor

copy editor turns article with changes back to editor

editor makes changes, turns in copy to art department

editor, editor in chief, art director discuss art and layout

art department prepares rough layout, plans art

art director assigns art

artist creates art

artist turns in art

art department prepares initial layout

editor reviews layout

editor approves layout

copy editor reads copy in layout form, returns changes to editor

editor approves changes, returns layout to art deparment

art department prepares new version of layout; places final art

copy editor re-reads story, makes final changes

art department produces final layout

managing editor, editor, copy editor, and art director approve final layout

files sent to service bureau/printer

service bureau/printer returns color proofs

editors and art deparment review proofs

proofs are approved

publication is printed

43

members of team: freelance writers, freelance artists, editor(s), copy editor(s), art director, HTML production department. In the web world, we can parallel many of the same steps—however, since the medium is different, changes may be reflected as so:

article is conceived by editorial team

article assigned to writer by editor

writer writes article

writer turns in article to editor

editor reads article and edits it

editor discusses article with art director

editor turns article over to copy editor

copy editor turns article with changes back to editor

editor makes changes, turns in copy to art deparment

editor, editor in chief, art director, and HTML director discuss art and layout

art department prepares rough layout on paper, plans art

art director assigns art

artist creates art

artist turns in art

art and HTML director prepares initial online layout

editor reviews layout

editor approves layout

copy editor reads copy in layout form, returns changes to editor

editor approves changes, returns layout to art department

HTML director prepares new version of layout; places final art

copy editor re-reads story, makes any final changes

HTML director produces final layout

managing editor, editor, copy editor, and art director approve final layout

HTML files tested on server

HTML files go live

If you're a one person "team," then your flow may go like this:

determine your story's content

write your story

re-read article and edit it

determine accompanying art

create art (or purchase clip art)

prepare initial online layout

review layout

re-read copy in layout form

make editorial changes

prepare new version of layout

review new version of layout

make any final changes

put files on server

test files off server

HTML files go live

summary

   If you're able to break your site down into a foundational scheme, you're well on your way to creating a functional overall design scheme. Taking the time to flow-chart your many ideas will not only help to create a navigational plan for your site, but help to break down the tasks at hand for a more manageable project overall. If you don't have the person-power to update your site on a daily basis, then don't include a page called "daily news." It doesn't mean you have to throw the idea away. But only include those elements that you can realistically do now within your schedule and budget.

CHAPTER 3

WORKFLOW

page properties

learning from what works in print

"The Universal is always the same,
the specifics are always different."

— Robert Aitken

Page elements, such as font sizes, colors, and other visual cues, serve as navigational and identifying cues to your viewers. Take a look at any typical magazine, book, or newsletter, and you'll notice that it has a distinctive logo or title, matching story or chapter title typefaces, and page numbers in the same place on every page. Once you've been a subscriber to the same magazine, you become familiar with what columns you want to read and where to find them, either by knowing in general what area of the magazine in which they can be found (news stories in the front, features in the middle, humor column on the last page), or by identifying the writer's picture, or even knowing where to find the page number in the table of contents—if the design has remained consistent for at least a few issues.

The same goes for web pages. While there are probably a lot of web publishers that don't consider their site a "magazine" or "newsletter" per se, successful navigation and familiarity with a site depends on the same basic visual features. Subtitles, or larger than–body–text type, tell you you're about to embark on a new section. Text under an image or photograph explains what the picture is all about. A page, section, or chapter number gives you a hint about where you stand in the whole puddle of pages.

nameplate/banner/logo

Generally the nameplate, banner, or logo of a site is the first and most prominent visual on the first page, and possibly subsequent pages. This identifying feature should be distinctive; it serves to establish a visual identity that viewers will (hopefully) remember.

If you have an existing business, your business logo is an obvious choice for the identifying banner of your web site. If you're a logo virgin, the rules of a good logo are that it's unique, that it's stylish but not too trendy (unless, of course, you're running a "trendy" oriented business), and

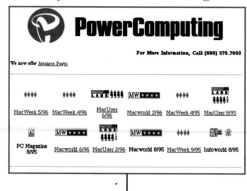

The Power Computing logo is the first thing to appear on its company site. If you know the logo, you know you've arrived.

most of all, communicates what you want the audience to know about you, your business, and your attitude.

Font choice is a little more difficult to push on a web audience, since the typeface displayed is a user-defined preference in most browsers. Netscape Navigator, for example, lets users override typestyle preferences. Even if you decide you want your body type to be Megalar Schoolbook Bold, the chances that all your viewers have this typeface is pretty weak.
You can, of course, make all of your type image files—but unless you also offer a text alternative, those unable or unwilling to view the images miss out on your content.

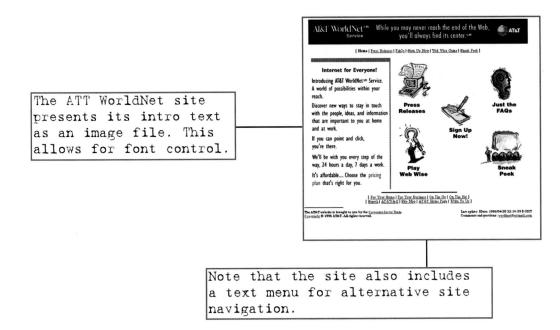

The ATT WorldNet site presents its intro text as an image file. This allows for font control.

Note that the site also includes a text menu for alternative site navigation.

What you do have control over is font size and attribution. Font size and attribution tags give the coder at least some control over what the viewer is looking at. For example:

<h1>Headline 1</h1><p>

<h2>Headline 2</h2><p>

<h3>Headline 3</h3><p>

<h4>Headline 4</h4><p>

49

<font size=1>really small type</font><p>

<font size=8>really big type</font>, and now it's back to its default size.<p>

Here's a <font color="#FF00FF">font in a specific color</font>, and now it's back to its original color.<p>

<pre>This is "prefor m   a   t   t e d" text, which reads any

                spacing you include while typing.</pre>

<code>Code also generally shows up as a monospaced typeface, but responds to other html tags more predictably.</code><p>

This is italics.<p>

This is bold.<p>

This has strong emphasis.<p>

<blink>This blinks.</blink>

These codes result in this, at least in the Netscape Navigator browser:

Just like during the early days of desktop publishing, when people suddenly had laser printers and tons of fonts at their disposal, we run the danger of using every font tag and attribute just because we can—and therefore, run the risk of a resulting "ransom note" effect. In other words, even if you can't use a lot of different fonts, try not to use every single attribution tag—it's too easy to make your page look messy and ugly if you use too many different ones on the same page.

JUST FOR FUN

Can you guess which
major company's logo
each one of these
spoofs? To test your
logo prowess, go to
http://www.prophetcomm.
com/prophetsite/
leggomylogo.html.

do you know your logos?

Visuals and logos, just like jingles and celebrity spokespeople, act as cues to remind us of a company. Our eyes see a stylized eye-ball icon, we know it stands for the CBS network. We see an upside-down peace sign, our brain

51

knows Mercedes. And unless you've been absent from the planet for a few years, you know that big yellow rounded–top "M" represents a semi–popular fast–food joint called McDonald's.

Advertising, marketing, and other corporate– and brand–identity firms thrive off the challenge of making memorable company logos. People don't have time to read a tome describing a company every time they want to buy a certain name–brand item.

Prophet Communications, a San Francisco–based communications firm, has presented us with a bit of a challenge—it's taken popular logos and replaced the actually company name with its company name. View an altered logo, make your choice of correct company, and if you're right, you're flooded with admiration and god–like idolatry. If you're wrong. . . well, let's just say you better learn how to turn on the TV.

statement of purpose

While this sounds very stiff and formal, some sort of statement of pur–pose helps your viewers to figure out not just why your site was created in the first place, but also why they should bother to hang out there at all. The statement of purpose should answer at least a few of the following questions:

who the site is for (i.e., people interested in art by Picasso)

what the site offers that's helpful and/or unique (i.e., quotes from friends or relatives of the artist about his/her work)

who you are and **why** you've decided to create the site

Think of this as writing the "objective" on a resume, or as the answer to "what do you have that eight million other sites don't have?"

Ziff-Davis Press puts the technology of the 21st century at your fingertips now. Whether you're hitting the keys for the first time or exploring every page of the web, Ziff-Davis Press has books, multimedia, and online products tailored to your needs. Let us be your guide to the information age. Our innovation makes it possible for you to enter the future now.

ZD Press presents its statomont of purpose at the very top of its home page, and tells us just who they think the site—and its prod–ucts—are for.

table of contents

The first thing I look for in a site or other publication with which I'm unfamiliar is some sort of table of contents, or "what you'll find on this site."

Tables of contents in books and newsletters are usually broken down in the order in which the chapters or stories fall. On a site, since there may not be a linear order to which people will follow links throughout, you're given the choice of creating lists sorted alphabetically, by category, by the order in which you want people to go through the site, or at random.

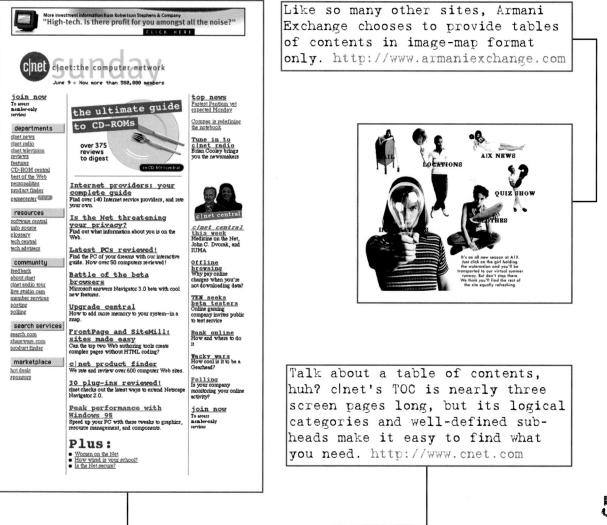

Like so many other sites, Armani Exchange chooses to provide tables of contents in image-map format only. http://www.armaniexchange.com

Talk about a table of contents, huh? c|net's TOC is nearly three screen pages long, but its logical categories and well-defined subheads make it easy to find what you need. http://www.cnet.com

53

publication information

The logo or banner mentioned previously is the first step in conveying information about your web site. If your site is a publication, or up-dated regularly, issue and volume information are helpful cues—as well as giving the impression of a professional site that continually offers something new (just make sure that you actually *do* offer something new!). You can either use the typical Issue 1, Volume 1 moniker, or a date label (i.e., March, 1996).

Other publication information is provided to tell viewers who's responsible for the site. This can take the form of a masthead (see page 55) or if your site has a name of its own, you'll want to inform viewers of the company or individual responsible for its implementation.

```
RETRO labels its
site overall by
month, and with-
in the daily
news section, it
informs the view-
er of the last
date on which
the section was
updated.
http://www.retroa
ctive.com
```

| Home Page | TELETYPE | RETROradio | Feature |
| Viewpoint | City Guide | Tip Tray | Discussions | Archive |

the daily RETRO news
Friday, June 7, 1996

TELETYPE

society
page

The Art Deco Society of San Francisco is a non-profit organization devoted to preservation, education and celebration of the period between the two World Wars. Even if you don't live in San Francisco, this is a wonderful organization to join for the newsletters and other information they provide, not to mention the camaraderie of fellow decophiles. Membership information is found on their spanking new website. For those in the Bay Area, the organization holds numerous elegant events during the year, including the Preservation Ball and the Gatsby Summer Afternoon. (6/7/96)

masthead/credits

Ah, the *masthead*, or the list of people who put together a site or publication. Self–indulgent? Well, it certainly can be. But this part of the site is not only potentially fun or annoying, it gives the site a face, a humanistic touch, and a feeling to viewers that there's actually someone out there behind the screen. Plus those who work on your site get to have a bit of fun putting together their own pages, or at least get a little pub–licity. If Bob Smith created a piece of art for your site, give Bob Smith a listing. Put in his picture. Link to his site.

```
ITP Review's extensive masthead
not only lists those persons
responsible for the site, but
also includes mailto: or home-
page links (to those who have
them) in order for viewers to
contact or find out more infor-
mation about those individuals.
```

contact information

Another incredibly important piece of info that's often missing from many commercial sites is basic contact information—especially if I'm actually interested in the product or service a page may be touting. What's the use of going to all this trouble of saying "buy me!" if you're not going to give me the chance to do so? The more info, the better, and if I'm on a product information page, I'd like the proper sales and/or informational contact at the company for that product.

Information to include:

- company name

- company address

- company phone number(s)

- company fax

- e-mail address(es) for appropriate information

- a list of key personnel and their relevant contact information

Even if your site isn't commercial, if you're encouraging people to write to you or contribute their feedback, give them a way to do so. A simple mailto: tag on the bottom of pages is all it takes.

kickers

Kickers are short blurbs that help to introduce a story or categorize a headline. For example, perhaps you have a number of stories on your site about wool yarn products, broken down by category, such as the following:

- Knitting

- Weaving

- Customer Yarns

● Profiles

● How To's

You've written a story about a customer called Fly Fishing with Wool Yarn. To help give readers a clearer mental categorization of just what this story is about, place a kicker above the headline, such as "Profile of a Customer" or "A Step-By-Step How To." You can see choosing one or the other of these gives a different impression of the overall purpose of the story; a profile versus a hands-on tutorial.

headlines

O.K., in five words or less, describe this chapter. Headlines are perhaps the most difficult and the most fun part of a story to write, because they must convey as much as possible without being too lengthy or vague.

The key tip for headline writing is to explain the benefit to the viewer. Note the difference among the following in a headline for a story about cooking eggplant:

Eggplant is Hard to Cook (negative connotation; no cure)

Don't Kill Yourself Cooking Eggplant (implies that there are easy ways to cook eggplant, but starts off with a negative phrase)

The tone of a story is successfully set with a good headline. SALON's headlines are well done, and convey the mood of the story, such as the tongue-in-cheek "Redneck Gays: Fightin' and Fornicatin' Down South ."

Eggplant Cooking the Easy Way! (positive connotation; benefit is that this story will make it easy)

5-Minute Eggplant Recipes (positive; time saving)

subheads/subtitles

If I took out all of the subheads in this chapter, you'd still be able to find out the same amount of information in the text, but it would take a lot longer to get to. Subheads break up otherwise extensive rants, and give viewers's eyes a place to rest, as well as serving as a navigational cue to what's found in a particular section.

lead-ins and pull-quotes

Lead-ins and pull-quotes are similar to kickers because they give hints as to what the main text is all about. Lead-ins are generally placed before the main body of text, while pull-quotes are placed within the body of text. Their benefits are two-fold: the foremost, giving viewers a brief overview or invitation into the main text, without forcing them to read the whole thing at once.

Pull-quotes and lead-ins can also offer graphical pizzazz to your story, helping to break up what otherwise may be pages of straight text. The easiest way to create a pull-quote or lead-in is to copy a witty or zappy sentence or quote from the main text, perhaps cutting it just enough to tease the reader into delving into the whole story.

SALON's use of lead-ins complements its headlines, and give us more of an idea of a story's innerds.

teasers

Hey, want to find out how to make a million dollars with your web site? How's that for a teaser? Teasers invite people into your site, either as text in the table of contents, as captions under photos, or as additional links under a related story. The teasers/links "Make a Million With Your Web Site", "A Profile of a Successful Web Master", or "Free HTML Software!" might follow a story about "Web Sites Made Easy" to lead readers through to other sections of the site.

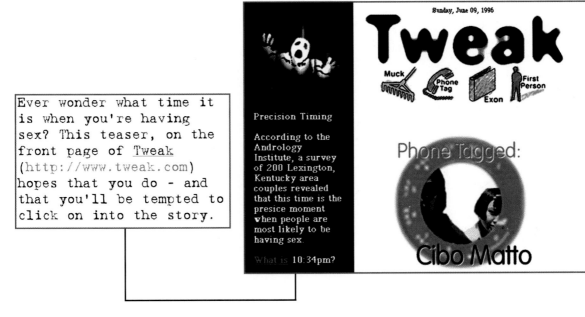

Ever wonder what time it is when you're having sex? This teaser, on the front page of Tweak (http://www.tweak.com) hopes that you do - and that you'll be tempted to click on into the story.

artwork/photographs

A picture can be worth a thousand words—as long as it's not a thousand K in size. Pictures are not only cool in their own right, but they can help lead a reader into a story, explain concepts that otherwise may take 10 pages to illustrate properly, or simply be eye candy for the masses.

The rules have to be followed with photos and other art—and the most important rule is to make them SMALL (see Graphic Appeal, beginning on page 161). I'm not talking small in square inches, but small in byte size. The smaller the better.

captions

Placement is key. A dominant piece of artwork or photo will tell your viewer where to look first. Simply pick one image that is proportionally larger than the other images to tell readers "This is where you should look first!"

Imagine a newspaper full of photos with no text underneath them to tell you what the picture's about. Like pull-quotes, captions also help to give viewers a capsule view of what's in a story, as well as describe what's going on in an image or photo.

Most images in the In Our Path site include concise captions that help to put the photos in context with each other and with the accompanying essays.

Click on the image to view detail.

© 1989 Jeff Gates

The circumstances of this pet's death can only be surmised. Reports of wild dog packs roaming the area were reported in the local media during the time of the injunction. Many believed these reports were exaggerated in order to force better maintenance of the Corridor.

jumplines

In magazines and newspapers, we're used to seeing "continued on page 14," and then following that cue to read the rest of the story. The cool thing about hypertext documents is that if your document does span more than one page, a simple click on the jumpline takes you right to the "top" of the next page. Generally, the jumpline on a web page is simply the word "next."

Similarly, we also see "continued from page two," giving us the cue that if the story first caught our eye while looking at page 14, we could go back to page two to get to the beginning. On web pages, jumplines could read "back" or "to the top," giving the navigational options to go back one page or to the very top of a story or section.

page numbers

Page numbers serve in a linear print publication to give you an idea of where you are in the reading process. Whether numbers, words, or icons, each page should provide some sort of clue to the viewer as to where they are in a section of a site or the site as a whole. To make navigation easier, placement of this cue should be in the same or similar area on each page.

summary

While you may not be publishing an online magazine, every web page can learn from the elements used in print publications to give viewers a sense of place, and provide navigational cues and visual stimulation.

Some tips for page elements:

Keep a checklist of each element you want on each page to remind you what you want to include.

Borrow from the pros: besides looking at sites you like, dig through your favorite magazines to get ideas for key page elements and navigational cues. Note how they separate chapters, how they write headlines and pull-quotes, how photos and illustrations complement the body text (and where they are placed on the page), and so on.

5 human-computer interfacing
familiarity breeds content

"The computer can't tell you the emotional story. It can give you the exact mathematical design, but what's missing is the eyebrows."

— Frank Zappa

Anyone who has ever designed a software application that has any sort of user intervention portion has played a part in human–computer interface development history. If you've created any sort of web site, then this means you, too. Perhaps some of these ventures haven't played a very crucial part, and they haven't turned the computer industry or the public on its ear, but there have been some that have. Take the introduction of the Macintosh operating system for instance, which then bred the rush to other visual operating systems such as Tandy's DeskMate, Geoworks, and Microsoft Windows for PCs.[1] Suddenly, floppy and hard disks are represented by disk icons, documents by symbolic electronic sheets of paper, directories look like tiny manila folders—or, at the very least, we could use menus and keyboard shortcuts to manipulate our files. We take these features for granted now, and most of us know what these symbols mean, and what will happen when we double-click on them.

The success of these iconic interfaces stems from the familiarity people have with the properties these symbols represent. A folder holds files. A trash bin is where you throw things away. And it's great that instead of having to type out archaic commands, we can click on a file and drag it from place to place. The programs that are most successful under these platforms are those that, for example, have similar functions that use the same command key combinations or can be found in similar menus, such as Save, Print, Select All, Undo, and so on. The more applications that conform to the basic familiar routines, the more intuitive they are to learn and navigate.

At a glance, we know what this sign means. It's no surprise, then, when its also used as a symbol to stop an action in your browser or other software. It's familiar, and most people can deduce what it means with no explanation.

Street and other where-to-go signs are non–computer examples of human interface design that works because of familiarity and standardization. It is probable that

[1] About the Macintosh graphical user interface: yes, I know that Xerox PARC did the graphical interface thing first, but it's Apple's Macintosh that started off the rush to make consumer-oriented computers graphically-inclined.

most people you know recognize the symbol for stop, restrooms, walk and don't walk—whether they are represented by color (red for stop), shape (stick person wearing a skirt for a women's bathroom, or the triangular shape of a yield sign), or another iconic form (blinking hand for don't walk; circle with a line through it for "don't do what's inside this circle").

use what you love, love what you use

In the office in which I worked back in the days when DOS–based programs ruled the world, there was great debate about whether WordStar or Microsoft Word was the best word processor to use. Neither one of them had a sexy interface, and both required that you either kept a 300–page reference nearby or memorized tons of key combinations to do something really difficult, like bolding text or centering. The truth was, both applications had something better than the other; both had features the other didn't. But because each had a steep learning curve (compared to word processors today, at least), it was the people who had gone through the trouble of learning the basic commands to get WordStar to double–space a document, or maybe get it to print out in (gasp!) Times Roman rather than Courier, that felt WordStar should be the standard application adopted by the office. The Word folks felt the same way for the same reason.

I use both Macintosh and Windows computers, and I can drive myself batty if I've been spending a lot of time using one and then go to use the other one. For example, Windows 95 has its "close box" in the upper right-hand corner of its windows—right where the Mac has its "resize" button. Invariably, I'll be working along merrily in Win 95 and decide to resize my window to full screen, and click on the close box instead, because I'm still in my Mac state of mind.

Ever noticed the little "home-row" bumps on your computer's keyboard? They're a favor to us touch typists so that we know where to place our fingers without looking at the keyboard—a form of touch-typist Braille if you will. Well, on a typical DOS/Windows keyboard, the bumps are on the letters F and J. On the Mac, they're on D and K. If I've been using my Windows machine, and switch to my Mac, I'll type "Ygr eubf ud viytdubh ygtiyhg nt

CHAPTER 5

INTERFACING

65

gsut,,," rather than "The wind is coursing through my hair..." before I know what's hit me. Is this bad interface design, or simply a mistake? I'm not sure—I just know that if I've just typed something that's complete gibberish, I'm annoyed. I'm sure there's a keyboard standards committee giggling their heads off because they've successfully foiled my sense of home-row familiarity and security.

Apple's CDAudio Player uses the same design and buttons as a "real" CD player. This familiar design makes it an intuitive application for those who have used a CD player, even for those not familiar with computers.

We become enamored with a certain program or a certain brand of VCR once we know how to use it to our advantage. Remember when ATM machines were a new, mysterious organism? Now we use them every day (unfortunately for my checking account balance), and we feel comfortable with almost any one worldwide that we are forced to withdraw from. Note, though, that there are still text instructions on each machine (in some places, in multiple languages) because there are so many different types of ATM kiosks. There is no standard among banks that say, for example that "green button = checking" or "square button = withdraw." If there were, and the public at large eventually knew that "green button = checking," then including elaborate text instructions might no longer be necessary. After all, stop signs merely say the word "stop." They don't have to say "STOP before you cross this white line to see if anyone is coming, or someone may run into you, or you may hit a pedestrian, and you will be arrested!"

becoming a successful interface designer

It's logical to conclude that if someone is comfortable getting around your site, they'll spend more time there, and enjoy the experience that much more. While web design and implementation isn't the same as developing, say, an ergonomic toaster, the basic human–thing interface rules apply. Namely, that as innovative or beautiful or zippy your site or appliance is, if it doesn't serve the person using it, it's no good.

And yes, we are at the mercy of whatever browser our viewers happen to be using. This we can't help. But we can make the information we present accessible in a familiar—yet unique—fashion.

Donald Norman, author of *The Design of Everyday Things*, stated in his interview for *The Art of Human-Computer Interface Design*, that "the first principle of human interface design, whether for a doorknob or a computer, is to keep in mind the human being who wants to use it. The technology is subservient to that goal." He then goes on to suggest that the ideal interface design team should include cognitive scientists ("or at least a psychologist or anthropologist"), programmers, and industrial designers.[2] Shall I wait here while you go back to school for 40 years?

Let's just face facts. Most of us, when faced with a web–design project, don't have this kind of team to play back–up for us, and I envy you immensely if you're both an HTML coder *and* a cognitive scientist. What we can fall back on is logic, our own experience with applications (and street signs, for that matter), and look at sites that we find intuitive to give us ideas that take us down the non–wayward road.

logic versus reality

Can we assume that all newbies to the web know that if a word is underlined it means that when it's clicked on, it will take them somewhere? Or that when they put their cursor over an image and it turns into a little pointing hand, that when they click, they'll be on their way to a new

[2]Interview with Donald Norman, *The Art of Human-Computer Interface Design*, edited by Brenda Laurel, © 1990 Apple Computer. Interview by Howard Rheingold. Addison Wesley, ISNB 0–201–51797–3.

experience? I really can't tell you for sure. What we can be relatively hopeful of, however, is that if they are using Macintosh or Windows or some other graphical operating system, they are used to clicking on icons to get things to happen. And people's familiarity with clicking is one reason that hypertext documents are so popular in the first place.

There are symbols that most computer users are used to, or will run across in nearly every application they'll use. One, for example is the question mark. Generally people know that they click there when they're thinking "I have questions, I need help!"

Other common navigational icons[3] include the following:

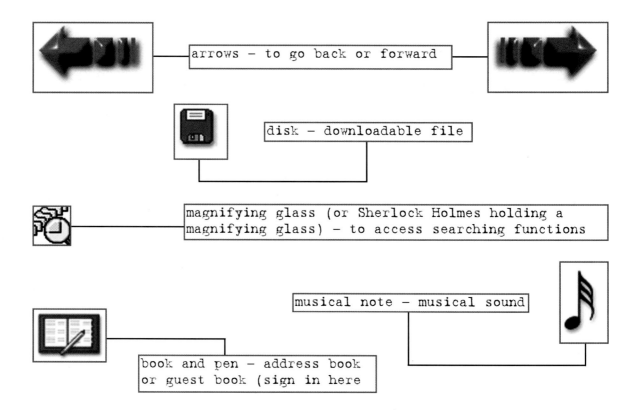

arrows – to go back or forward

disk – downloadable file

magnifying glass (or Sherlock Holmes holding a magnifying glass) – to access searching functions

musical note – musical sound

book and pen – address book or guest book (sign in here

The Netscape Navigator tool bar, when set up to show pictures or both pictures and text, utilizes many of the icons that we may be used to using in other applications: the front and back arrow, a house to go "home" (in this

---

[3] Arrows, music, and disk icons courtesy of Laurie McCanna, author of *Creating Great Web Graphics.* Download them for free non-commerical use from http://www.mccannas.com.

Additional icons courtesy of Jay Boersma, available from Barry's Clip Art Server, http://ns2.clever.net/~graphics/clip_art/clipart.html.

case, to go back to whatever page you've set up as the default home page in the browser), a printer for printing the page, binoculars for searching, and a stop sign for stopping a page from loading. Icons that we probably haven't seen in other applications, such as the reload icon and the open icon, have the text underneath to show us what the image stands for—and the application, before you start customizing your options, defaults to the view of both pictures and text to help familiarize new users with the icon's actions.

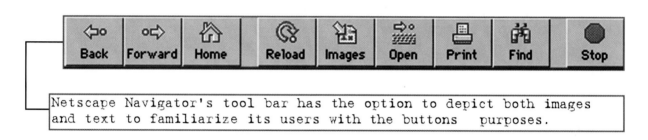

Netscape Navigator's tool bar has the option to depict both images and text to familiarize its users with the buttons purposes.

Familiar icons are all well and good—but what if you want to use something different? Let's say I use the following image on my page:

What does this icon mean? If I don't tell you what it means, what do you deduce will happen when you click on it? A picture like this is hard to interpret. Is the boy crying or sweating because he's singing so loud? Is he pretending to be a warrior with a pot for a helmet, and proclaiming victory over his victims, or did his older sister shove the saucepan on his head, and now he's crying because he can't get it off?

Besides this, what kind of area will you be going into when you click on this icon? Of course, your deductions may be a little easier if you know the angle of my web site. If I tell you the name of my site is "Children's Songs," you may think it's more likely that he's singing. If I say its "Mean Things Kids Do," then you'll probably come up with something close to the sister-and-the-saucepan scenario.

If I tell you when you enter my site that this boy means "send me e-mail," even if the image has nothing to do with e-mail whatsoever, at least now you know what it means and what will happen if you choose to click it. If at any point I change my icons, or change their meanings in the middle of the site to mean "download a file"—even if I tell you—I'm bound to frustrate or lose you altogether.

iconic imagery

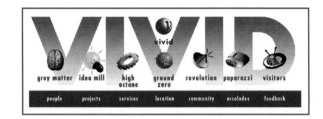

So what happens to the game plan when a site—in this case, VIVID (http://www.vivid.com/)—uses a brain to represent a link to information about the people behind the company? Does this make sense? Am I, as a new user of this site, going to know that a brain icon means people? (not if you're where I'm from, but that's another story). Luckily, VIVID, and many other well-designed sites, add a couple of words that help to discern the icon from any misrepresentation.

Take a look at a few other site navigational menu bars. Note that each icon is accompanied by a one- or two-word explanation for its purpose:

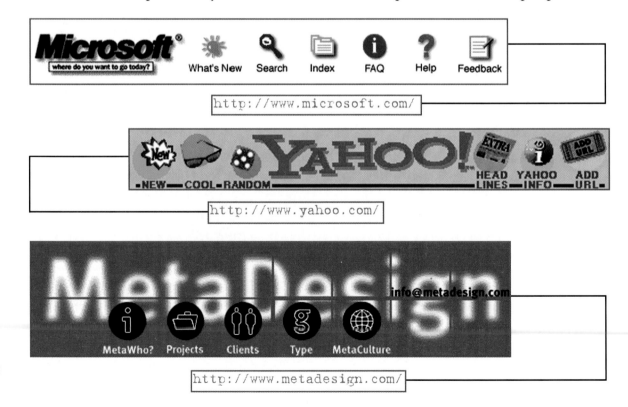

Everyone wants their site to look different from the other guy's. If all web sites had exactly the same icons, it would be a very boring place. If you're using original icons that could be interpreted any strange way possible, take a hint from your computer's desktop—try adding a word or two of explanation to an icon's design, or add a hypertext link next to the icon that explains its meaning. If you hate the idea of spoiling your icons with words, perhaps try an easily accessible, separate "how to navigate our site" or "what our icons mean" page that people can link to from any main page of your site. I like to think that most people aren't stupid. But a lot of them can get lost easily, and it's your job to prevent this from happening.

If you do bother to describe your standard or non-standard icons, make sure your one- or two- word descriptions make sense. If I have a recipe site, and I label an icon of a cowboy boot as "French poodles," what does that mean? A useless explanation is just that.

metaphorically speaking

The definition of "metaphor" is "*n.* a figure of speech in which the context demands that word or phrase not be taken literally, as *the sun is smiling*; a comparison that doesn't use *like* or *as*." "Life is *like* a box of chocolates" is a simile, because it compares one thing to another using the word "like." If the saying were "Life *is* a box of chocolates," it would be a metaphor.

Generally, in visual design, people define metaphor as a familiar image that portrays actions or activities that work similarly to the physical product represented.

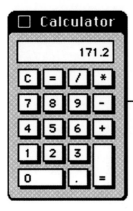

Computer software plays on metaphor to represent software functions in a way that we find familiar in our tangible world. If we've used a physical calculator, we can probably figure out Apple's calculator without instructions.

Hence, the "metaphor" of a computer's desktop with its pieces of "paper," file folders—or software (like contact managers or calculators) that look like their tangible counterparts. Metaphorically, they *are* their tangible counterparts.

71

CHAPTER 5

INTERFACING

On the web, we see metaphor being used in sites like Star Trek: Voyager, in which the main theme throughout the site is that you are a Star Trek officer who wakes up with amnesia, and you must figure out your mission, information about your co–officers, and so on, before returning to active duty. Upon arrival at the site, new visitors are ordered to go to sickbay immediately. "Oh, good. You're awake." is the first thing you're greeted with as you enter sickbay. The doctor then "hands" you a PADD (or personal access display device—sort of like the 34th century's version of the Newton), which gives you access to the ship's databases—Mission, Personnel, Technology, Comm Stations, Earth Support—and includes an "Evaluation" that you must complete in order to return to duty. If you pass the evaluation, you'll be rewarded with having your name added to the U.S.S. Voyager Honorary Crew Archives. Once back on duty, you can then use your PADD to access updates about "your mission," such as info about previous and upcoming episodes.

Paramount's Official Star Trek: Voyager site (http://voyager.paramount.com/VoyagerIntro.html) uses its own sickbay and "personal access display device" – or PADD – for its navigational and informational metaphor. In this site, you are a crew member, and the PADD is your way of getting around and finding out information.

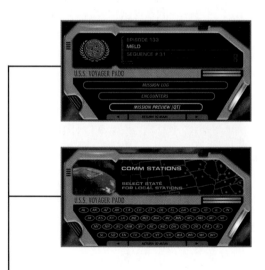

The Star Trek: Voyager PADD metaphor is carried successfully throughout the site, using the device to display help menus, mission information, and access to affiliate stations nationwide.

relevant metaphor

When choosing a metaphor for your site, try to make it relevant. The Star Trek: Voyager metaphor obviously has something to do with the show. If you sell gardening equipment and supplies, what if you set up your site as a garden? Imagine rows of vegetables (click on a carrot to go to carrot seeds, recipes on carrots, and carrot growing tips), hoes and wheelbarrow nearby (click to purchase gardening tools, tips on how to care for tools, and how to pick the right tool for the right job), bugs crawling on a plant (click to find out how to get rid of bad bugs; find out which bugs are good and which are bad), a cloud and sun (click to find out about growing seasons; best placement of plants), dirt (click to find out about soil requirements; how to test your soil; purchase fertilizer), and so on.

the 3 c's: consistency, consistency, consistency

On the web, good navigational design weighs its success heavily on consistency. Roger Parker, author of the best-selling *Looking Good in Print* states that "Style reflects on the way you handle elements that come up again and again. Part of a document's style is decided from the beginning. The rest emerges as the document develops visually.

"Consistency is a matter of detail. It involves using restraint in choosing typefaces and type sizes, and using the same spacing throughout your document."[3]

While Parker's book was written in 1983, and deals with only the paper medium of communication, his point stands true today. My point is that you needn't use the same icons or layout as everyone else—but you must be consistent within your site so that people know that if they click on a banana icon on one page, it takes them to the same place if they click on the same banana icon on another page.

[3]*Looking Good in Print: A Guide to Basic Design for Desktop Publishing*, Third Edition, by Roger Parker. © 1993 Roger Parker. Ventana Communications Group, Inc. ISBN 1-56604-047-7.

Then there's location, location, location. Icon and navigational text should always be placed in the same place, or as close as possible, on every page. It's frustrating to have to search around a page to find the navigational cues; i.e., a menu bar on the top or left on some pages; on the bottom or right on others.

> TIP: USER TESTED, VISITOR APPROVED
>
> If you've been working on your site day in and day out for a long while, take a break and let someone else look at it for a while. Invite constructive criticisms. How easy is it for your tester(s) to get around? Do they know what your icons and headlines mean what they'll be getting into if they click on them? If they've clicked through multiple layers, how hard is it for them to get back to the top of the site, or to another area? Your impromptu "usability lab" will probably surprise you and has the potential to be of great assistance in your overall design and the flow of your site.

summary

Have I mentioned consistency? As a designer, you're responsible for creating an environment in which viewers will find themselves clicking through with ease. Whether you choose stereotypical icons to represent actions or design your own, you must stick with your plan, and explain where necessary, even if it may seem obvious to you.

The goal here is to make the experience as independent from the limits of the web and its browsers as possible—to communicate your message and your information in as painless and seamless a way as possible. Pay attention to the little details so your visitors won't find them glaring inhibitors to their navigation.

page layout

structured layout versus free-form

"I don't know anything about music.
In my line you don't have to."

— Elvis Presley

75

I think by now we've all kind of noticed that publishing on the web is a bit different than publishing on paper. But there are a number of tips we can pick up from basic on–paper design schools–of–thought that are helpful in putting together storyboards and page layouts.

Do you remember back in first grade when you first started learning to write letters? Do you remember those lines in your workbook that showed you how tall your capital letters should be, and the dotted lines between them that served as reminders of where your lowercase letter should reach? Even in our adult lives, we use lined notebook paper to help us write neatly rather than in squiggles that wander hither and thither. These lines serve as visual guides to help keep our handwriting in check.

Many traditional designers use grids and guides to help lay out pages in an attractive manner. You'll notice that when you look at a newspaper, newsletter, or magazine, if it is laid out in columns, they tend to be of a uniform width with uniform space between each column.

Chances are, the designer used a grid to lay out these pages. Many well-known page–layout programs, such as Adobe PageMaker and Quark XPress,

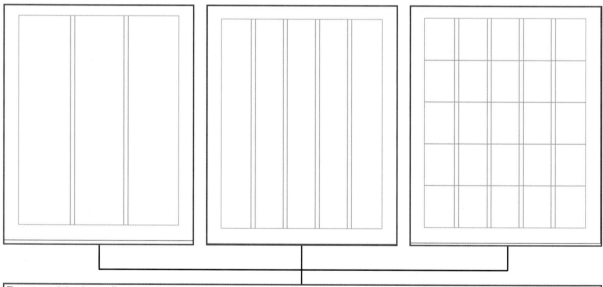

In traditional page design, column guides and grid lines are usually used to assist the designer in aligning blocks of text and images, whether they use old-fashioned paste-up or a high-end layout application such as PageMaker or XPress. These examples show a three-column, five-column, and a five-column with a split-up-into-five-equal-spaces vertical grid.

enable you to set up columns and use grid lines to help you align blocks of text and images.

Although HTML editing applications and the browsers that view their results have a long way to reach the layout functionality of Quark XPress (at least at the time I'm writing this chapter), we can take advantage of grids to conceptualize our ideas for the final site page layouts.

grids as guidance, not gods

The word "grid" sounds so rigid—and its definition is dry and uninspiring: "n. an arrangement of regularly spaced bars; the system of intersecting parallel lines that divide maps, charts, and aerial photographs, used as a reference for locating points." You may get the impression that because I suggest using grids to lay out your page, you're going to end up with pages that look blocky and inflexible. While this is certainly a possibility, grids can actually be more flexible than you might think.

One thing I have to stress before we go on is that grids are to be used as a guidance tool to help give a page balance, and to maintain consistency among a number of pages. I don't feel that it is necessary to follow a grid's lines to the exact pixel in order to make a web design great, but using grids will assist in the visualization and planning of aspects of your page, such as where you will place text on each page, where graphics will be placed, or where columns fall in relation to one other.

Grids are extremely helpful in determining how big a graphic should be, or in helping the viewer's eye to be guided through a page, rather than distracted by an image or column of text that just doesn't quite seem to lay right.

The following example is an imaginary print newsletter layout in which I show how I use grids to assist me in laying out print material. Note that I've used the five-column grid pictured previously—but I don't simply use the five columns I set up literally; I don't just let the text flow from one column to the next to the next, and so on. For one thing, unless I'm printing on very big paper or using very small text, the columns would break after a couple of words, and it would be difficult to read and look rather strange.

flexing the grid: an example

First, let's take a look at the headline. The word "typo" spreads across four columns, and takes up one-fifth of the print area.

Both the volume notification and the word "news" take up two of the five columns. The volume notification aligns with the top of the top-fifth section of the page; "news" sits on the same base-line as the word "typo" - along the bottom of the top-fifth section. Together, the words "typo" and "news" take up the entire five columns.

The vertical bar of gray fills one column.

volume 1 issue 1

typo

news

by Crystal Waters meow

ALSO IN THIS ISSUE:
the web goes to the dogs.....page 3

WHAT KIND OF PERSON creates a web page for their cat? Of course, you haven't - or have you? It's ok, you can admit it. One of the most written-about sites on the web is called "Talk to my Cat," a site that let's you type in a message to some guy's cat, who apparently is sitting next to the computer listening to it translate your words into sounds it understands (because, of course, cats can't read). Then there's the plethora of cat pixs, drawings and poetry. Why are we so obsessed with our cats?

"As a matter of fact, cat's are usually cooler than people."

It doesn't matter why, really. Now that we have this web thing to afford us unlimited space to show off and talk about our cats, why should we care why?

Cats are just plain cool. As a matter of fact, they are usually cooler than people. Ergo, I advocate that everyone should put their cat on the web, and service providers should give anyone who does so all the free web space they can eat. As a cat owner, this sounds incredibly fair to me. *(cont. p. 2)*

meow

Internet, below left, and Gandalf, right, are two of the coolest cats on the web.

cool

on the

cats web

The main body of the text doesn't follow a straight column down the page, but it does use the column guides to keep the balance and proportion of the text consistent. In this case, I started out by spreading the text over four columns; in order to fit in the image and the pull-quote, the text then flows into two columns. Further on down, below the pull-quote, I let the text flow back out into the first column, making it then three columns wide.

The teaser, or mini-table of contents "Also in this issue," is boxed into three of the five columns.

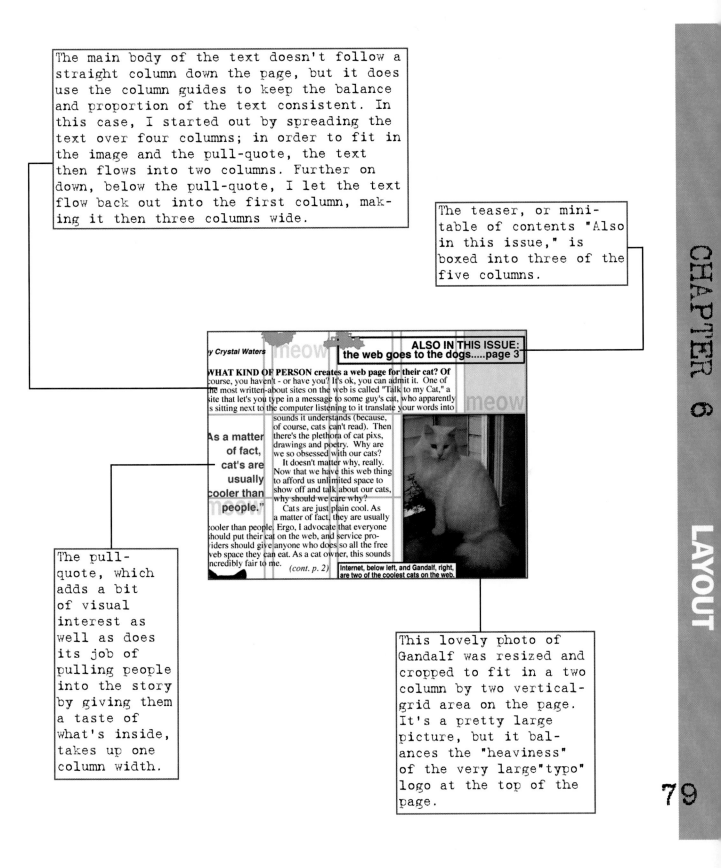

y Crystal Waters

ALSO IN THIS ISSUE:
the web goes to the dogs.....page 3

WHAT KIND OF PERSON creates a web page for their cat? Of course, you haven't - or have you? It's ok, you can admit it. One of the most written-about sites on the web is called "Talk to my Cat," a site that let's you type in a message to some guy's cat, who apparently is sitting next to the computer listening to it translate your words into sounds it understands (because, of course, cats can't read). Then there's the plethora of cat pixs, drawings and poetry. Why are we so obsessed with our cats?

It doesn't matter why, really. Now that we have this web thing to afford us unlimited space to show off and talk about our cats, why should we care why?

Cats are just plain cool. As a matter of fact, they are usually cooler than people. Ergo, I advocate that everyone should put their cat on the web, and service providers should give anyone who does so all the free web space they can eat. As a cat owner, this sounds incredibly fair to me. *(cont. p. 2)*

"As a matter of fact, cat's are usually cooler than people."

Internet, below left, and Gandalf, right, are two of the coolest cats on the web.

The pull-quote, which adds a bit of visual interest as well as does its job of pulling people into the story by giving them a taste of what's inside, takes up one column width.

This lovely photo of Gandalf was resized and cropped to fit in a two column by two vertical-grid area on the page. It's a pretty large picture, but it balances the "heaviness" of the very large "typo" logo at the top of the page.

CHAPTER 6   LAYOUT

I added a vertical line on the left margin, up to the fourth horizontal guideline, which helps to separate the body from the headline.

My gorgeous cat Internet's ears peek up over the bottom fifth grid line, but I included a line behind him to separate the upper four-fifths of the page from the headline he's serving to grace. Notice that he's sitting on the guideline for the bottom fifth of the page - which is also where the baseline for the large letters that are placed on top of him sit. (If I had placed him with his front paws in alignment with the baseline, it would have appeared that he was sitting up in the air, disconnected from the text).

incredibly fair to me.   *(cont. p. 2)*   Internet, below left, and Gandalf, right, are two of the coolest cats on the web.

cool **cats** on the **web**

The headline for this cover story, "Cool Cats on the Web," doesn't reach all the way across the page - but it appears to, because I added Internet's picture behind the text. I did, however, use the column guide to determine the space between the words "cat" and "web," and made the word "web" two columns wide on purpose.

Note that the entire text body and the teaser serve to fill up the three middle fifths of the page vertically, although the only content in those three vertical rows that strictly follows a vertical line is the photo of Gandalf the cat. I placed the pull–quote below the blue line rather than aligning it per–fectly with the top of Gandalf's picture to avoid looking too "griddy." The words "on the" in the "Cool Cats on the Web" headline are two columns wide, but I moved them to a random position over the words "cats" and "web" to make it a little more visually interesting.

The caption for the two cat images is also two columns wide, like Gandalf's photo. I chose to offset it to the left of the image, lined up within the third and fourth columns.

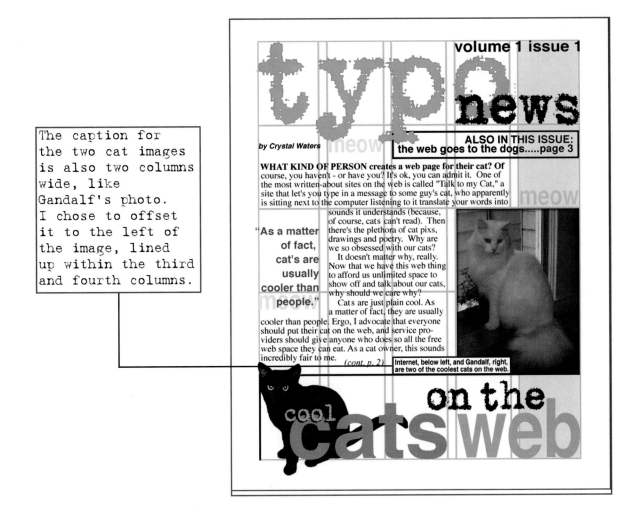

web layout differences

As I mentioned before, controlling web layout is a bit more difficult than controlling a paper layout. For one thing, if there are no tags inserted that control where text will break, the text will flow and wrap at whatever width the viewer happens to have the browser window sized to.

```
Here are three shots of the same paragraph, and the
effect of the browser window size on the way the text
will fall. I didn't include tags to control the place-
ment of the text, so the text conforms to the width of
my browser window. The middle image is how the text
looks on the default Navigator for the Mac window size.
```

```
Crystalwaters.com is too much to type anyway. Too
much of a chance to make a mistake when trying to
link to me. So I tried the simple approach. I'd
pick a word that was easy to remember, easy to
spell, and would roll lusciously off the public's
tongue like word-, suck-, or meat-dot-com -- all
sites that not only have received kudos from
around the world, I like them, too. And they're
fun to say. Go ahead, repeat after me:
suck-dot-com. suck-dot-com. suck-dot-com.
```

```
Crystalwaters.com is too much to type anyway. Too much of a chance to make a
mistake when trying to link to me. So I tried the simple approach. I'd pick a
word that was easy to remember, easy to spell, and would roll lusciously off
the public's tongue like word-, suck-, or meat-dot-com -- all sites that not
only have received kudos from around the world, I like them, too. And they're
fun to say. Go ahead, repeat after me: suck-dot-com. suck-dot-com.
suck-dot-com.
```

```
Crystalwaters.com is too much to type anyway. Too much of a chance to make a mistake when trying to
link to me. So I tried the simple approach. I'd pick a word that was easy to remember, easy to spell,
and would roll lusciously off the public's tongue like word-, suck-, or meat-dot-com -- all sites
that not only have received kudos from around the world, I like them, too. And they're fun to say. Go
ahead, repeat after me: suck-dot-com. suck-dot-com. suck-dot-com.
```

There's also the fact that the average default browser window on a 14-inch monitor (still the most popular monitor size) is smaller than a standard paper page size—not to mention that a monitor shows us a landscape layout (wider than it is tall), rather than a portrait layout (taller than it is wide), as most paper pages are viewed.

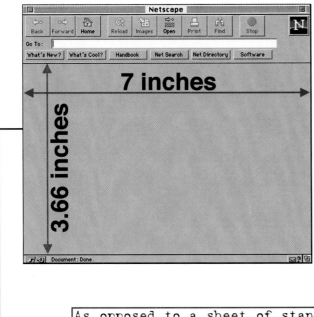

It's difficult to take a layout that was designed for print and translate it literally to the web, but with luck and a little patience, you can get pretty close.

```
As opposed to a sheet of standard paper, the default
Netscape Navigator window that comes up on my 14-inch
Mac monitor leaves very little space in which to design
a page. It's also wider than it is tall, the opposite
of a standard newsletter or book design.
```

the bigger, the scrollier

What happens if your page is too big to fit on one small little web browser window? Scroll bars appear, either on the right-hand side of your window (to scroll up and down on a page), on the bottom of the page (to scroll back and forth horizontally), or on both, depending on the direction the page overflows over the size of the browser window. There's also that little resize-your-window box that's on the lower right-hand corner of the browser window that's easy enough to drag down or over to make the browser window wider or longer.

Scrolling is easy. Resizing a window is easy. But before you design your site to any old size assuming that everyone will happily scroll along to find whatever it is that's hidden beyond the browser boundaries, know this: nearly everyone I've talked to about web site navigation finds it annoying as hell to be forced to scroll all over the place or resize a window to suit the designer's whim (by the way, many of the people I talked to were designers; check out some of the related pet peeves beginning on page 237). Make your viewers do it too much in your site to get to the information they want, and they will feel that you've somehow taken advantage of them, or don't really care how you're controlling their viewing experience.

There are a few sites that use scrolling as part of the experience of their site, and if it's done well, this forced moving-around stuff doesn't annoy because at least the experience is visually satisfying or intriguing in its execution within the medium.

J.Walter Thompson site,
http://www.jwtworld.com/tableaul.shtml, uses a
horizontal-scrolling format for its introductory page.

applying grids to web layout

Chances are, I'm not going to be able to remake my newsletter on the web in perfectly duplicated form—unless, of course, I take a screen shot of the entire page and stick it up as a graphic or image map—which may be a pain in the neck for people to download because I would have to maintain a pretty big image size to make the page readable.

I was, however, able to get it pretty close to my paper five-column layout—and at least got it to fit horizontally in the smallest web page default width.

Before I began the layout, I determined just how many pixels wide I wanted the page to be, and then subtracted 10 pixels from each side to account for the browser window margin. In this case, the browser window is 488 pixels wide, so I had a working area of 468 pixels. Because I wanted a five-column grid balance, I then subtracted 40 more pixels from the working area—since there are four column dividers in a five-column page, and I wanted the space between my columns to be 10 pixels wide. I end up with 428.

When I divide 428 by five, I get 85.6 pixels. This is how wide each individual column will be.

In general, I made all the images smaller because the page is proportionally smaller, and I want to save my viewers precious download time. So for the most part, I made all images one column width smaller than they were in the print version.

When I determined that I wanted the typo news logo to spread across four column widths, I multiplied 85.6 by 4, and added 30 (for the three column dividers the image crosses). I came up with 372.4, and rounded down to 372 pixels (note: there may be situations where you want to be more precise than having to round up and down. In my example, I don't have to be that fussy.). The three column-wide Cool Cats on the Web banner on the bottom left calculation went like this: 85.6 x 3 = 256.8 + 20 = 276.8. I rounded up to 277 pixels, and made the image that wide in my graphics program.

The gray fifth column is a one-pixel high background tile that is 1200 pixels wide (so that if someone has a really big monitor, they won't get a repeating tile horizontally). I started the gray on the tile at pixel 382 (85.6 times 4, plus 40 in this case, to put the edge of the bar within the fifth column).

To get the volume 1 issue 1 text to line up with the background gray band in the fifth column, I added a one-pixel GIF and changed its WIDTH tag to equal 312 pixels. I didn't do any fancy calculations; I added and subtracted pixels until it lined up where I wanted it to. Note that I used text for this part rather than keeping it as part of the image, because it's something that I'll be updating with each issue.

```
<IMG SRC="./tab.gif" ALIGN=LEFT WIDTH="312" HEIGHT="1"
BORDER="0"><FONT SIZE=+1><STRONG>volume 1 issue
1</STRONG><FONT><BR>
```

The 372-pixel typo news logo takes up four "columns" of space.

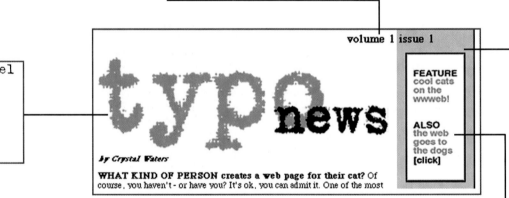

For easier placement and to use up some of the fifth-column space (which was used by the logo in the print version), I made the "in this issue" box vertical for my web page. Its tag comes above the typo news logo so that the text aligns right. I added 10 pixels of vertical space so that it wasn't butting up against the volume/issue number.

```
<IMG SRC="./also.gif" ALT="also in this issue" ALIGN=RIGHT
WIDTH="74" HEIGHT="157" BORDER="0" VSPACE="10"><BR><IMG
SRC="./typonews.gif" ALT="typo news logo" WIDTH="372" HEIGHT="128"
BORDER="0"><BR>
```

The pull-quote is a column-width image.

```
<IMG SRC="./pullqt.gif" ALIGN=LEFT WIDTH="86"
HEIGHT="103" BORDER="0" VSPACE="10">
```

The text simply wraps around the pictures and falls into its four-column, two-column, three-column format automatically.

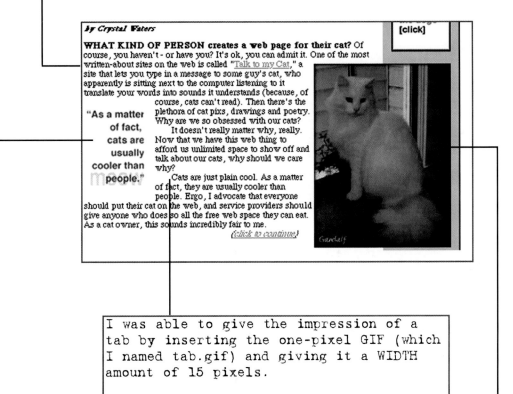

I was able to give the impression of a tab by inserting the one-pixel GIF (which I named tab.gif) and giving it a WIDTH amount of 15 pixels.

```
<IMG SRC="./tab.gif" ALIGN=LEFT WIDTH="15"
HEIGHT="1" BORDER="0">
```

Gandalf's picture is now two columns wide, or 85.6 times 2, plus 10 pixels. I added five pixels of VSPACE to offset text a bit from the bottom and top of the image. Its tag was added just before the third line of text.

```
<IMG SRC="./gandalf.jpg" ALIGN=RIGHT WIDTH="181" HEIGHT="234" BOR-
DER="0" VSPACE="5">
```

CHAPTER 6 LAYOUT

Using the same trick as I did with the volume/issue number, I've inserted the one pixel GIF and added width to its tag until the "continued" line was where I wanted it to be.

As mentioned previously, I calculated that this image should be 277 pixels wide to fill three columns. However, I added 10 pixels of white to the right edge of the Cool Cats on the Web image so that the caption under the photo would line up with the bottom of the Gandalf photograph (because the text is aligning left to the Cool Cats image).

Rather than a graphic caption, I went with this text caption so that I could easily link to Internet's and Gandalf's pages, and so I could update captions in future issues more quickly.

TIP: A NOTE ABOUT PDF

PDF, or Portable Document Format, is a format developed by Adobe Systems Incorporated to allow the transfer and viewing of documents among different platforms. Using Adobe Acrobat, you can basically save out any document in any software (such as an Excel spreadsheet, or a PageMaker newsletter) to PDF format. Anyone with the Adobe Acrobat reader (available, free, for Macintosh, Windows, HP-UX, SunOS, and Solaris platforms) can open your document and view it as you've designed it, with your images, fonts, and layout. Using the Weblink plug-in, creators of PDF files can include URL links within PDF documents. When a viewer is looking at the PDF document, and clicks on an URL link, Acrobat Reader will launch the viewer's browser and take them to that site.

Many sites have offered PDF files for download from their sites that you could then open with Acrobat Reader (or use Reader as a helper file, which would be launched automatically once a PDF file was downloaded); with newer versions of browsers and Acrobat appearing as I write this, however, it will be possible to use Acrobat files basically as web pages - embedded in a browser window - if the browser supports the Adobe Acrobat plug in.

To keep up on the latest developments with PDF and Acrobat, head to http://www.adobe.com/acrobat/.

applying grids to web layout

The benefit to using tables or frames tags in your page designs is that it gives you more control over where things will appear on your viewers'

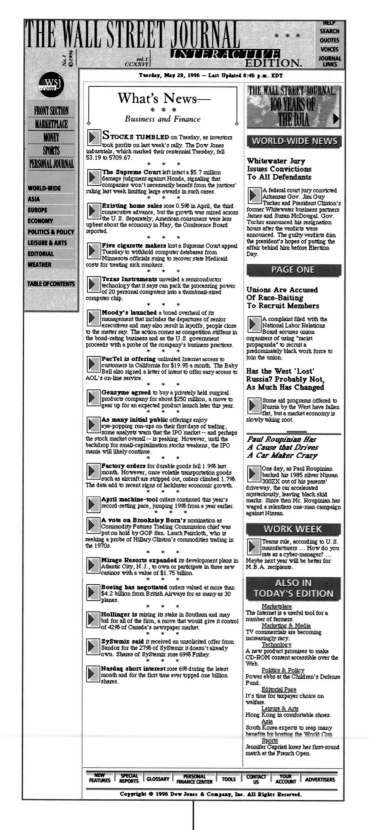

browsers—that is, if your viewers are using a browser that supports tables and frames. If you're determined to use a strict layout, then tables and frames are two solutions. Some would argue, however, that the word "solution" is much too strong of a word, because tables can sometimes have a mind of their own, and most of the uses of frames on web pages out there are just butt-ugly.

Tables, however, are a good choice for those sites such as BookWire (http://www.bookwire.com/) and *The Wall Street Journal* (http://wsjournal.com/) because they have the potential to successfully imitate print versions of a newsletter or newspaper.

The Wall Street Journal uses tables to effectively mimic its paper version.

BookWire's site uses tables with borders on to separate and align sections of its extensive site.

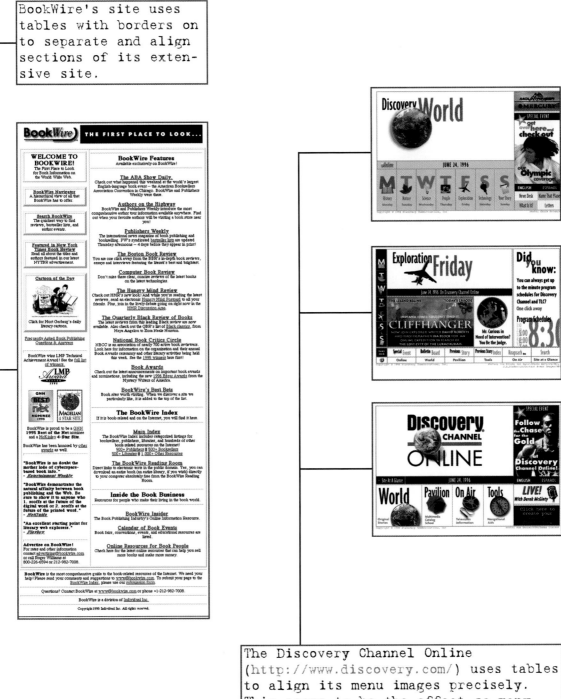

The Discovery Channel Online (http://www.discovery.com/) uses tables to align its menu images precisely. This seems to be the effect so many are trying to achieve with frames. Hey, why bother when tables can look this good?

It's a struggle to find sites that use frames well. My favorite use of frames is found on the Triple W Ranch site (http://ubinfo.pub.buffalo.edu/Chuck/) —mostly because the frames aren't obvious (i.e., no scroll bars; no more frames than are necessary). If frames are used in an unobtrusive way such as this, then I say go for it.

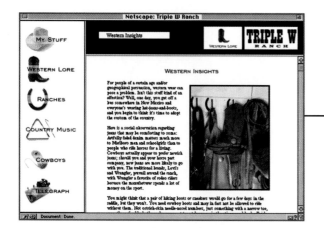

The Triple W Ranch site uses frames to organize and present its content effectively and unobtrusively.

The official Sony PlayStation site (http://www.scea.sony.com/SCEA/findex.html) offers a framed-based layout that obviously follows a set grid. While most of the frames include looping animations or random images that slow down the overall loading time of the page, it's still an intriguing example.

The official Sony Play-Station site uses a six (horizontal) by five (vertical) block grid as the basis for its framed-base layout.

using images to control a page layout

Another way that is often used to control how a page looks is through images—generally utilized as an image map for navigational purposes.

The New York Times uses images–as–image maps in its introductory pages, and these not only look like the headlines in the paper version, but serve to control the layout of the columnar layout.

Other sites use images for layout purposes—but instead of using them as image maps, they are created using images for the sake of presentation only.

The New York Times uses images as image maps to give its site the look of its printed paper.

This page from the story "Holy Smoke" by Stephen Berg, hosted on the word site (http://www.word.com/), is laid out in a columnar format using GIF images for the text. Also note how this site uses the effective and somewhat unique horizontal scrolling layout.

free-form layout

And what if you want to design a site with absolutely no obvious format or planned-out layout? Well, lucky for us all, anyone can lay out any page any way they please, and it seems that most do. My table of contents for my site wasn't planned out using any sort of grid; I simply spaced stuff out and moved stuff around until they were where I wanted them to be. Two of my favorite page layouts on my own site weren't planned out at all.

On the typo menu page, I used the <PRE></PRE> tag to space out each menu item. The <PRE> tag reads anything you type literally, so if I type a space then a period, then two spaces, then a period, etc., it puts those items in that exact place.

```
<PRE><font size=4>                   . . . . . <font size=3 color="#999966">week of June 9 - 15, 1996  [1.16]
<font size=4>
          <A HREF="./new.html">what's <font size=6>new</font> this week</A>        <a href="../week/week.html">week link</a>
   . . <a href="../talent/talent.html">talent for rent</a>           . . . . . . .            <a href="../technoid/technoid.html">technoid</a>
          <a href="../gallery/gallery.html">gallery</a>                          .                        .
          .              <a href="../homage/homage.html">homages</a>                  .
<A HREF="./jobs.html">job board</A>              <a href="../cool/cool.html">cool connections</a>       . .
          <a href="../writings/writings.html">writings</a>
          <a href="../pix/pix.html">random pix</a>        . . . . . . . <A HREF="./kudos.html">ego feed</A>
          . . . . <a href="../crystal/crystal.html">my biostuff</a>                              .

          <A HREF="./wcd/wcd.html">the <font size=6>web</font> <font size=6>concept</font> & <font size=6>design</font> book</A>
</PRE>
```

Here's the code for the typo menu page. Notice how the spaces and characters I've typed correlate to the resulting page.

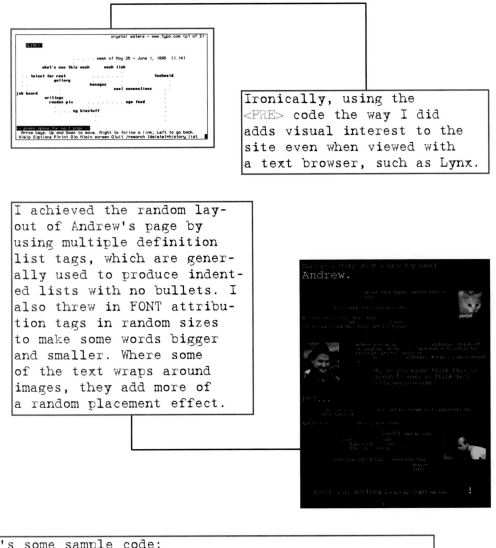

Ironically, using the <PRE> code the way I did adds visual interest to the site even when viewed with a text browser, such as Lynx.

I achieved the random layout of Andrew's page by using multiple definition list tags, which are generally used to produce indented lists with no bullets. I also threw in FONT attribution tags in random sizes to make some words bigger and smaller. Where some of the text wraps around images, they add more of a random placement effect.

Here's some sample code:

```
<P>
<A HREF="./gandalf.html"><IMG SRC="./gand.gif" ALIGN=RIGHT
WIDTH="72" HEIGHT="74" BORDER="0"></A>
<DL><DL><DL><DL><DL>
Among other things, Andrew likes to play <A
HREF="http://www.yahoo.com/Recreation/Games/Card_Games
/Magic__The_Gathering/">Magic: The Gathering</A>.
</DL></DL></DL></DL></DL>
<P>
<DL><DL><DL>
He recently got a new roommate, <FONT SIZE=6><A HREF=".
/gandalf.html">Gandalf</A></FONT>.
</DL></DL></DL>
<P>
```

CHAPTER 6 LAYOUT

95

summary

While paper–page layouts and web–page layouts have distinct differences and challenges, we can use traditional design tools and tricks to help us conceptualize and lay out web pages. Tables and frames can assist in the layout of structured pages, as long as their presence doesn't distract from the overall design of the page.

The basic overall "rule" of designing a layout, when it comes right down to it, is if you like how it looks, and it doesn't inhibit navigation or ease of use, then go with what appeals to you. Try to stay within the boundaries of the limits of web page and monitor dimensions, unless you have a very intriguing layout, such as the J. Walter Thompson site, mentioned earlier. Scrolling for entertainment, or as part of the artistic–web–experience, is one thing. If your site is dedicated to information exchange, scrolling for little reward becomes tiring.

storyboarding & conception

visualizing the pages to be: examples & case studies

"Everyone wants to be Cary Grant.
Even I want to be Cary Grant."

— Cary Grant

97

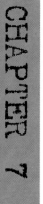

Storyboarding is a process that is used in the planning of sequential projects, such as movies, animations, comic strips, multimedia presentations, or anything that shows action or connections among different aspects of the project.

He thought it was just going to be another normal kitty day...

..when suddenly, a MOUSE ran across the floor!

His heart racing, he froze as the creature turned to face him...

This storyboard portrays a series of actions among — and positions of — characters. Creating storyboards for your site helps to conceptualize both the layout of each page, as well as the relationship of pages to one another.

In the case of a web site, storyboarding serves to help plan and visualize both the page layouts of each page, as well as to get an idea of the three-dimensional navigation and relations throughout the site. Just as an animator may draw out a storyboard of sequences for a cartoon to get a feel for the action and placement of its characters, a storyboard of a site gives you the "feel" of the lay of the land and how people will view and move through it.

Before storyboarding your site, it's a good idea to have at least a bit of background of some tools used in basic page design, so I hope you read (or at least skimmed over) the previous chapter. This way, you'll be able to conceptualize how images and text will relate to one another on the page in a practical, easy–to–navigate, easy–to–update method.

All those index cards you created to organize the content of your site will now expand into visual representations of your pages that will assist in content organization, page design, and navigational aspects of your site on a page by page basis.

You can either storyboard your site by sketching out pages on paper, or by creating prototype screens in HTML or in a graphics program. Either way, you'll probably end up rearranging things multiple times, recoding pages like crazy, trying both simple and quite complicated designs—and inevitably, detesting your site and starting the design over from scratch.

gamespot: the view behind a commercial site

On May 1, 1996, a new site hit the web. Big deal, right? Well, not a real big deal for most of us, since new sites hit the web every day... every hour... sometimes it seems like every minute. But the staff at GameSpot (http//www.gamespot.com/) had endured many long, long days furiously working away to launch its heavily promoted, soon-to-be-launched site. The "pre-site" had long posted the date and time it was going to hit: May 1, 12:00 noon, P.S.T. When the launch hour of noon that day came and went, and the site still wasn't live, a clever coder added the caveat to the site's announcement: "We meant Polynesian Standard Time!"–which of course, gave them a whole three extra hours to pound out the rough spots. Although the first deadline of many (its content is updated daily) was missed by a few hours, GameSpot has since seemed to hold true to its promises and overall reader and business missions. It has done so through trial and error, prototype and perseverance, tossing a pixel here and a pixel there–not to mention, many stages of pre-launch pressure.

GameSpot, a high-intensity
PC gamers web magazine, in
its final form.

With the help of Vince Broady, GameSpot's Editorial Director, I was able to get a few peeks into the process in which this new online PC gaming magazine site came into play. Broady is in charge of the site's structure, interface, and content, and manages a full-fledged editorial department and numerous freelancers and contributors. He's also responsible for making sure that the site is constantly up to date and maintains its mission statement and goals. In his words, "our mission is to be the world's single-best source for information about PC games." It's no small issue to try for the title of "world's best," and Broady explains how he and his team were (and are) constantly on their toes to try to reach the top–from the conception of their site, which contributed to the efficiency of its day-to-day updates and maintenance.

GameSpot's editorial goal, according to Broady, is "unlike most product-oriented publications": it's not meant to tell the reader what to buy. "Instead, our goal is to provide them with enough information–from the manufacturer, from our editors, and from other users–to make the buying decision that's best for them. We also seek to enable users to get the most out of the products they already own, to enlighten and entertain, and to constantly amaze our users with the depth, quantity, and quality of our coverage."

To do so, GameSpot's designers had to incorporate not only sections for each game in which on-staff reviewers rant and rave about products, but there is also a section on each product's page for the game's company to give their scoop, and an area in which site visitors are encouraged to add their two cents.

GameSpot's review pages incorporate areas in which the game company, the sites reviewers, and site visitors input their views about and experiences with a product. Each page also includes game ratings and stats, such as system requirements, release date, and price.

Broady also states that the magazine's business goal is to do all of these things and make money at it—"by delivering an ever-increasing, highly-responsive, and highly-targeted audience to their advertising sponsors." Its parent company, SpotMedia Communications, hopes to replicate GameSpot's model with a family of online publications.

> GameSpot is a commercial venture, and its ad index shows it's successful at marketing its audience to the appropriate advertisers. The site was designed to fit most ad banners, and its ads appear randomly on those pages that have them (most do). The ad index, shown here, sports advertisers banners—with links—so if readers miss the click opportunity for an ad that caught their eye, they'll be able to find all the current sponsors in one place.

When asked how they determined who GameSpot's market/target audience was, Broady told me that they had looked at a number of markets as potential targets for an online publication. "We chose PC games primarily because [we believed there were] glaring inefficiencies in the delivery of game information via existing vehicles, specifically print magazines."

The browser a viewer is using can greatly determine the way a site is layed out. In GameSpot's case, since it covers Windows and DOS games only, the priority was to design for those users. Because the site is still relatively new, Broady is unsure of what browsers most of GameSpot's visitors are using. "There's really no way to know with any degree of certainty which browsers your audience is using until you're able to ask them, so in the beginning you're basically forced to make an intelligent guess. Obviously, different browsers have different capabilities, and it is very difficult to create a compelling design that can be displayed on all of them."

Its market determined the layout and dimensions of GameSpot's pages. Since its regular viewers are interested in PC games, most of which nowadays demand fast processors, high-resolution monitors, and quality sound boards, the site is designed for those who have the equipment to handle the games requirements as well as the browser requirements.

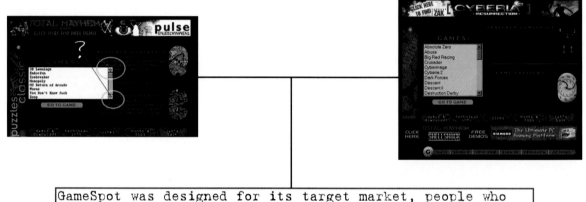

GameSpot was designed for its target market, people who use Windows machines and high-resolution monitors to play games. This is evident when the site is viewed on a Macintosh—at least with a standard 14-inch monitor. Note how on the Mac, GameSpot's games list (in the center white block of text) cuts into the text to the right. On the PC, these section intros lay out as intended, using the default font for forms and proper spacing.

"We made a decision not to allow our design to be determined by the lowest common denominator," says Broady, "but instead to take advantage of features which are available on the most popular browsers, which we determined to be Netscape 1.2 and 2.0, and Internet Explorer 2.0. While this excludes some portion of the market, we believe that in the end the quality of our design is critical to our success, and so the trade-off is worth it."

He adds, however, that GameSpot is in the process of designing a "low band" version of its site. This site will have lower-bandwidth graphics for those with less-capable browsers and slower-than-28.8K access to the web.

While Broady came up with the overall structure of the site, such as how information is organized and presented, the navigational interface was a group effort. The site's look and feel was created by an outside firm, CL!CK Active Media (http://www.clickmedia.com/), a team that created game-related sites for Virgin, Pulse, and Trilobyte. Broady states that the site is continually evolving as they learn more about the ways people are moving through it.

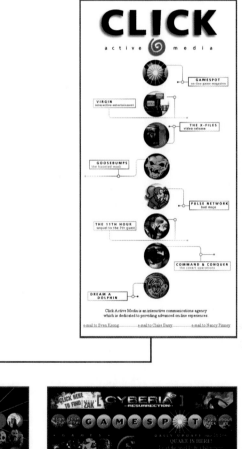

The CL!CK Active Media team that created the design for GameSpot, also created a number of other great-looking but modem-speed-hungry sites, such as The Pulse Network (http://www.pulsenetwork.com/), and the games Command & Conquer (http://www.westwood.com/covertops/index.html) and 11th Hour (http://www.vie.com/prodinfo/11th/).

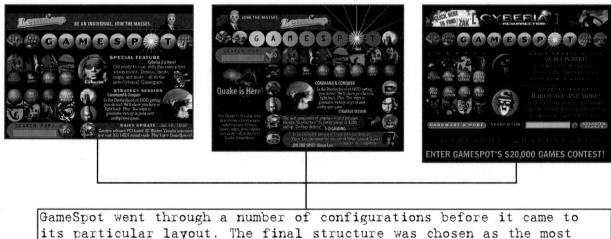

GameSpot went through a number of configurations before it came to its particular layout. The final structure was chosen as the most navigable and the most visually suitable for its image and for the sake of its users.

103

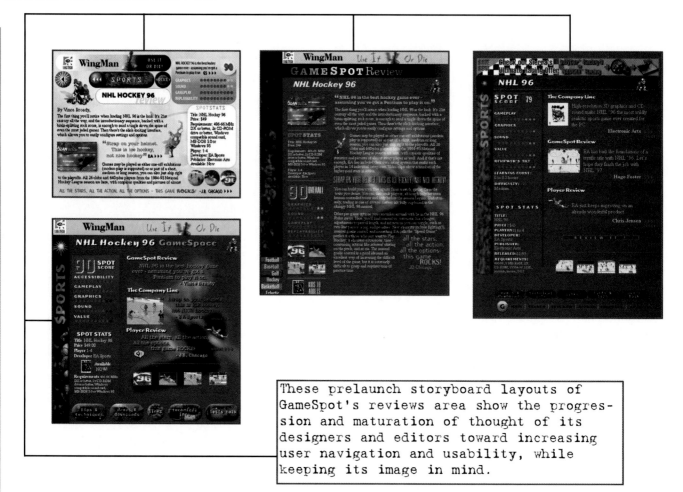

These prelaunch storyboard layouts of GameSpot's reviews area show the progression and maturation of thought of its designers and editors toward increasing user navigation and usability, while keeping its image in mind.

in our path: a different structure

In Our Path, a photojournalistic site covering the building of a Los Angeles freeway (http://www.tmn.com/iop/index.html), took a different turn in its conception. Its creator, Jeff Gates, wasn't thinking of a specific target audience as he was creating the site; instead, he tackled the project because he "wanted to turn a photo documentary into a hypermedia project that would use the special qualities of 'non–linear' navigation to enhance the documentary and story behind the project. What is wonderful about this medium is that it allows you to structure a project which allows the viewer to approach the issues from multiple viewpoints."

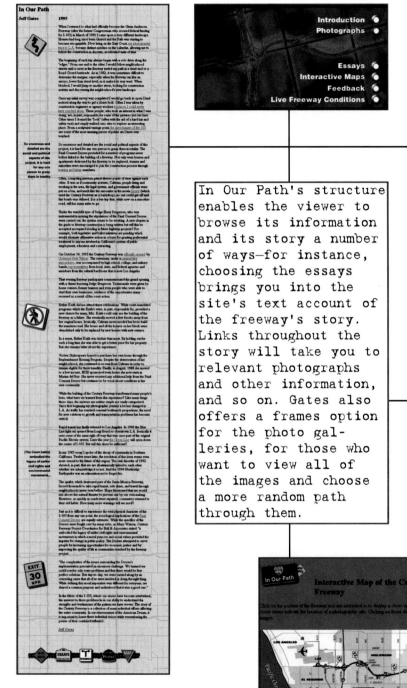

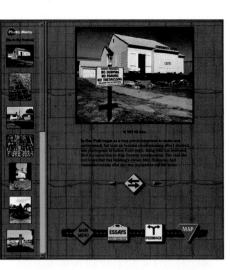

In Our Path's structure enables the viewer to browse its information and its story a number of ways—for instance, choosing the essays brings you into the site's text account of the freeway's story. Links throughout the story will take you to relevant photographs and other information, and so on. Gates also offers a frames option for the photo galleries, for those who want to view all of the images and choose a more random path through them.

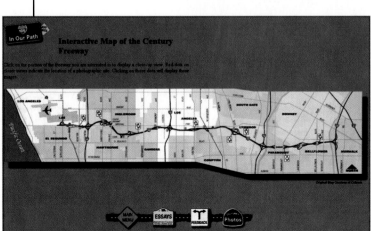

CHAPTER 7

STORYBOARDS

At first, Gates thought his audience might be those involved in the arts or interested in transportation. However, he then realized that he should also be targeting environmental issues, as well as more general "socially based" people and sites. "The web actually allowed me to discover new audiences and begin targeting them," Gates says.

The interface, which Gates designed, is meant for viewing in Netscape Navigator 2.0. He did, however, make sure that any features he used from Netscape's 2.0 tag set were backward compatible to those using Netscape 1.1. One important feature he includes–and uses–is the sites feedback capabilities. The dynamic part of In Our Path, in the Feedback area, uses a web-based conferencing system to enable viewers to discuss the work and site, and issues surrounding public works projects. It enables artists who are working in this area to post images from their own work and/or to link to their own sites.

Designing areas or even simple mailto:s for viewer feedback is crucial in the layout of your site. In Our Path uses a conferencing area to bring together those who are interested in the various subject matters touched on in the site.

Gates wants to make the interface logical and easy to navigate, and listens to what his visitors have to say. "Since the web allows for immediate access between the author and viewer, I have received suggestions from my audience as to how to improve the interface–which I did."

"Specifically, this had to do with how one viewed the photographs in the series. On one day, I received e-mail from two different people (one a photographer and one a slide librarian at a university) outlining the same problem: when they were viewing the images, they didn't know where they were in the linear flow of the work; that is, how many images were left to view. I redesigned the site so that those viewing without frames could see from the title on each page where they were (6/20, 7/20, etc.)."

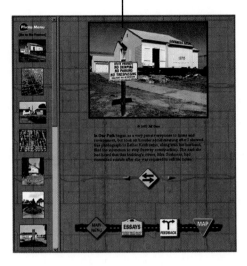

Frames give In Our Path viewers the option of choosing among the many photographs that are available in Gate's site. There's also a no-frames version for those without frames-capable browsers.

Gates chose frames (as he says, "judiciously and with a good deal of sensitivity to good design") to enable viewers to see thumbnails of all the images so they are able to view them in any order they want. The layout of both the frames area and the "regular" area are purposefully linked to one another to give viewers the choice of how to access the site's information.

summary

It's difficult to picture the overall navigation and feel of your site if you don't spend some time either drawing pages out by hand or testing various layouts in HTML. Keeping your audience in mind–especially regarding their computer abilities and interest in the subject–is crucial. There's nothing wrong with designing for a specific browser if you know that's what your audience is using; if you're not sure what they're using, then offer viewing options.

Designing the structure, either of pages or a whole site, can be wonderful–and frustrating–because of the many different ways a page can be layed out or linked to other areas. Yes, we're limited by HTML. But the "three-dimensionality" of a site can be used to our advantage if we've planned out a site's internal structure in a logical, usable manner.

CHAPTER 7

STORYBOARDS

107

mood lighting

choose the colors that best portray your image

"What is the color of wind?"

— Zen koan

Remember when getting your "colors read" was a hot business and magazine story topic? Suddenly, we could define ourselves as "warm autumn," and we knew exactly what color clothing we could get away with wearing, and those shades that best accentuated our skin, hair, and eye colors. (I'm a "cool winter," by the way...)

The colors you use on your site may not make or break you, but they definitely help to convey an image or a mood. Before you choose colors, it's helpful to consider color harmonies, contrasts, and what the combination may convey to your audience.

For example, think of how we use color in conversation to describe states of mind and being:

"feeling blue"

"in the pink"

"mellow yellow"

"green with envy"

"caught red-handed"

"told a little white lie"

We have established "rules" for colors in our wardrobe: light colors in summer, dark in winter; white for weddings, black for funerals (in the West, in any case); red roses for love, daisies for friendship. As times change, different colors and color patterns become acceptable: bright blue eye shadow one era and "natural" tones another. Tie-die shirts vs. GAP pastel pocket tees. Some of us are t-shirt and jeans types of people, and some of us wear only pinstripe. We define ourselves by our clothing, our cars, our furniture choices, and our web site's colors can emit the same "aura."

red means stop; green means go

Why do we associate red with "stop" and green with "go?" A stop-light's cerebral affect on us is not something we spend time analyzing when we drive up to it; we just do what it says because it's something we just seem to have known since we could first perceive things around us. People also associate red with "hot" and blue with "cold," just look at any water heater/cooler. Because we were brought up with the association, as politically correct as we want to be, we still tend to associate blue with boys and pink for girls (ever seen a blue Barbie box?).

Here's a list of common associations with common colors:

red

hot	stop	aggression	lushness (red velvet)
error	warning	fire	daring

pink

female	cute	cotton–candy

orange

warm	autumnal	Halloween

yellow

happy	sunny	cheerful	slow down
caution			

brown

warm	fall	dirty

green

envy	jealousy	a novice	spring–like (fertile)
pastoral			

blue

peaceful	water	sad	male

purple

royal	a stupid dinosaur

black

	evil	ghostly	death	fear	mourning
	night				

gray

	overcast		gloom		old age

white

	virginal	clean		innocent		cold

JUST FOR FUN

Did you know that when you say it with flowers, that red carnations send the message "My heart aches for you" or "admiration," and yellow carnations stand for "You have disappointed me" or "rejection"? For a list of what particular flowers and their colors symbolize, go to the 1-800 Flowers site, and read the page "The Language of Flowers" in the Enter Our Garden area. (http://www.1800flowers.com/)

Color theory and harmony and the affects of colors on mood, and so on, are fields many artists and psychologists have been studying for a long time, and there have been extensive studies and papers and books and lectures on the topic—far too many to site examples of every one (see sidebar for resources, though, if you'd like read up on more of the actual methods of color study).

A key point about color theory is that it's called color theory for a reason—there are no rules. Chances are you aren't going to need to read up on the reasons a room painted a certain color of blue will make you feel a certain way, or why food product packaging tends to have a lot of the color red in them, in order to create a good web page. There's also other aspects of a page, such as layout, images, and text choices, that will obviously make a big difference in the overall image of a site.

There are a few definitions you should become familiar with, since you're sure to run into them if you're planning on working with any sort of image manipulation program, such as Photoshop, or if you plan on reading up on color in general. If you have a design or art background, you've probably already studied this stuff 'til dawn, but here they are for the rest of us:

hue

The color attribute identified by color names, such as "red" or "yellow."

value

The degree or lightness or darkness of a color.

saturation

The relative purity of a color; also referred to as intensity. The "brighter" the intensity of a color, the more saturated it is. New jeans are saturated with blue; faded ones are less saturated blue.

chromatic hues

All colors other than black, white, and gray.

neutral colors

A black, white, or gray; otherwise known as "non-chromatic hues."

monochromatic

A color combination based on variations of value and saturation of a single hue.

Now that we're armed with these facts and theories, it's time to figure out how to pick a color scheme that works, is easy to read, and helps to put across the image you want your site to portray. By perusing through sites that use color schemes to their advantage, you'll be able to more vigorously pursue the right scheme for your own site.

text and background contrast

Here's the default color scheme in Netscape 2.0.

Text color is black, on a gray background.

Link color is bright blue.

Visited links are a shade of purple.

Here's a look at the default
colors in the Netscape Navigator browser. These colors aren't that inspiring,
but at least they are easily readable.

Of course, a site needs to have more than one color (how else could you read the text?). Most browsers support custom text colors, as well as custom link and visited link colors. The default color scheme for Netscape is a gray background with black text, blue links, and purple visited links. While this color scheme is good for read–ing, it's also pretty boring, which is why it's tempting to change it.

Studies show that the best color scheme for reading is black text on a white background, which is why you might have noticed that most books and magazines are printed with black text on white paper. Black text on white paper is high contrast, and high contrast is easier to read than low contrast.

Yes, there really are sites that use this
kind of color scheme. Amazing that anyone
sticks around to read them, huh?

These two colors actually
complement each other well,
but are not a good combination for background and
text because low contrast
makes it difficult to read.

Here's a color combination that
definitely contrasts, but large
amounts of text in this color
on this background could eventually be hard on the eyes.
This type of contrast can make
text seemingly "jump" or quiver
on the page.

This color scheme offers contrast, but is
it really that much easier to read? Perhaps.

But it's certainly not that enjoyable for
reading great amounts of text.

== Internet Casino ==
== Magic 8-Ball #1 ==
== Magic 8-Ball #2 ==
== Rock & Roll Hall of Fame and Museum ==
== Rock Music Quiz ==
== The Internet Adaptor Information ==
== Interactive Body Piercing ==
== Microsoft Product Information ==
== The Ultimate Band List ==
== Net Life! ==
== Elvis Spotter's Page ==

```
This is part of a screen shot from a page that uses an
impossible-to-read color combination. If it weren't for
the black equal-sign markings on either side of the
links, you'd hardly know they were there. Even the usage
of larger-than-standard text doesn't help readability.
Would you go back to this page?
```

Call me crazy, but if someone goes to the trouble of creating a web page that is difficult or impossible to read, it proves they don't care about their viewers. And I don't go back, unless I desperately need information from that site that I can't get anywhere else, and I've changed my browser's preferences to use the colors I wish to use to view pages. For more on text readability, see the chapter on Type & Style, beginning on page 145.

before you color, check the crayons

There's a little something that web designers affectionately (and sometimes not so affectionately) dub the browser–safe color palette. I became familiar with this palette when Lynda Weinman, author of *Designing Web Graphics*, told me about discovering the 216–color palette when she was writing that book's *Fun with Hex* chapter.

CHAPTER 8

MOOD LIGHTING

115

While you're obviously welcome to chose any colors your monitor will handle, browser–safe colors are guaranteed not to dither. Dithering is what happens when a color is not available in the palette, and the browser tries to compensate by combining pixels of other colors to accommodate. Here's an example:

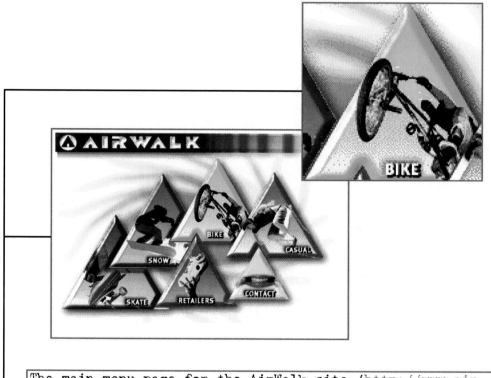

The main menu page for the AirWalk site (http://www.air-walk.com) displays dithered colors on my Mac Netscape screen. Notice in the closeup (actual size, actually) how the colors seem scattered and spotty.

Dithered colors look spotty or rough, while browser–safe colors retain smoothness on screen. To get the best effects, choose colors from the browser–safe palette for your images and backgrounds. This will be helpful when trying to match up image or background tile colors with text colors, or image colors with background colors. If you create an image in Photoshop, for example, and it consists of the RGB values of R=255, G=051, and B=051, you can match it up with the hex value that you may use in your HTML code for the background color or one of the text colors (in this case, #FF3333).

TIP: BETTER SAFE THAN DITHERED

For easy access to browser-safe colors, go to
http://www.lynda.com/hex.html and download one or
both of the browser-safe color palettes (one is
arranged by hue; one by value). Open up the palette
in the art program of your choice, and use the eye-dropper
tool to select the browser-safe colors as you need them.

Lynda's FTP site (ftp://luna.bearnet.com/pub/lynda/)
also provides
these images
for download,
as well as a
color lookup
table (CLUT,
show at right)
for loading in-
to your Photo-
shop Swatches
palette.

effective color combinations

The following sites are some of those I feel successfully use color in effective ways to support or portray an image. Notice how each site tends to be consistent with its color choices, or at least consistent with the over-all mood of the site. As you look at each page, try to pay attention to where your eyes go first. Is there a high-contrasting logo or image or icon that pulls your eyes to it? Where does your eye go next?

lush/rich

Sotheby's—http://www.sothebys.com/

It's rare for me to find sites that use red backgrounds that are both easy on the eyes and says a lot about a site's image. Sotheby's uses rich red-on-red and green-on-green color schemes that successfully put forth the richness of a velvet backdrop. Like walking into an expensive jewelry store, we are presented with a dark-yet-lush background that best allows the product to shine. Low contrasts among the colors helps keep the site subdued. If Sotheby's had chosen to have bright yellow or blue patches of text or background, it would have changed the overall feeling to be somewhat clowny.

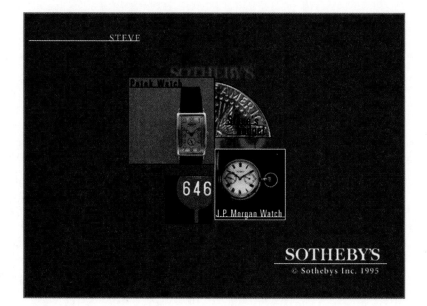

Ben, purposeful and proud, leaves the
subway at 68th and Lex and treads
with measured pace towards his destination.

His intent is clear, a claret of the finest grade

(no burgundy will do).

To celebrate an exciting new development.

A rebirth, it occurs to him, not just a birth.

Welcome to SOTHEBY'S

Information
News
Frequently Asked Questions
Departments and Experts
Ordering Catalogues
 & Publications
Sotheby's International Realty

Auction Adventures

Featured Sales: Auctions   Collector's
Keeping Time   538   Corner
Fit for a Sword   For the Connoisseur
The Heart of Scottish Art   Featured Appraisal: A True Story
                                          Emerging Collector
Highlighted Auctions   Notes for the Beginning Collector
Worldwide Calendar   Caring for Your Collection
Gallery of Past Auctions   How to Assess Value
Auction Results   Internet Resources
                                          Educational Programs

CONDITION

estimate

SOTHEBY'S
© Sothebys inc. 1995

lon
DON   ex
           HIBITION

AUCTION
309

AMANDA
BUDGET

10:02a.m. Amanda and Richard push
through the doors of Sotheby's to view the
exhibition for that week's Collonade Sale of
furniture. They are after a dining table they
glimpsed in their now dog-eared catalogue. It
is to be the centerpiece of their first home.
They are determined it will be theirs.

SOTHEBY'S
© Sothebys Inc. 1995

CHAPTER 8   MOOD LIGHTING

playful/lighthearted

Toy Story (Disney)—http://www.disney.com/ToyStory/

The use of bright primary colors and high contrast reflects the playful nature of the Toy Story site and the movie it supports. The toys are happy and bright and shiny, just like the colors of real toys—eye–catching for kids and adults alike. The white background sets off the bright foreground colors.

TOY STORY MAIN CHARACTERS

WOODY VS. BUZZ

businesslike

Oracle—http://www.oracle.com/

Oracle's site has a straight-ahead business look. Notice how even though most of the opening page is covered with a sort of dusty green, the first thing your eye falls on is the bright red line between the "n" and the "c". The buttons on the right-hand side then call our attention to the active parts of the image map.

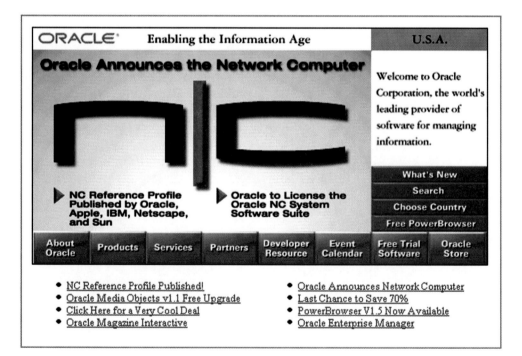

staid

H&R Block—http://www.handrblock.com/

No fooling around here; H&R Block's site is pin-stripe through and through. The white background (and lots of it) gives a clean appearance, with dark blue images and text portraying a no-nonsense approach to serious money handling. Note when moving on to the H&R Block Tax services that the color scheme turns patriotic on us—perhaps the red, white, and blue will inspire us to feel better about doing our taxes a little earlier next year. The Canadian part of the site loses the American flag scheme in favor of mellow greens, and the Executive area takes on a mahogany "briefcase" look.

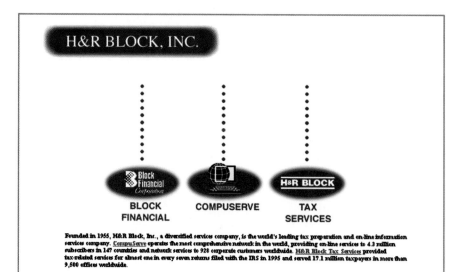

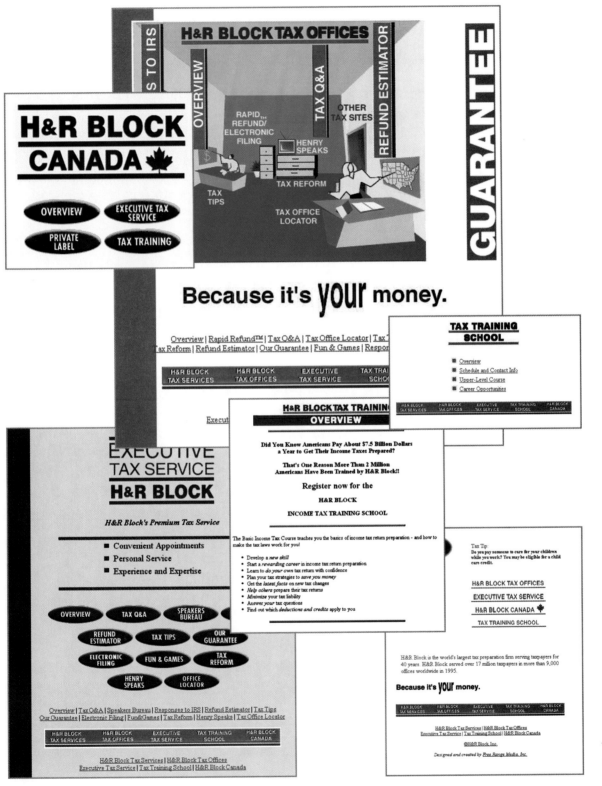

cheerful

1–800 Flowers—http://www.1800flowers.com/

Need a little tickler to brighten up your day? 1–800 Flowers' bright white background complemented by cheerful primary–color flowers and lots of bright greenery definitely portrays the happy image of giving and receiving flowers. The color combinations change appropriately to the colors we associate with different holidays (red for Valentine's Day), times of year ("autumn" colors for fall), and occasions (bright values for birthdays; subtle values for sympathy).

Pomp and Circumstance Bouquet

A special graduation deserves special recognition. One of our designers will create this striking arrangement featuring a combination of the finest premium long stem fresh cut flowers. The arrangement in a lovely glass vase will include flowers such as lilies, oncidium orchids, stargazers, roses and gerbera daisies.

retro

RETRO—http://www.retroactive.com/

Whether discussing Hawaiian cruise–ship menus, or those vices we swear off every New Years day, RETRO's color scheme successfully gives a feel of the retro–American–era its site is all about. Clicking into RETRO is like stepping into my Aunt Babe's living room when I was a kid. All RETRO needs is some clear plastic covers so that it doesn't get dusty.

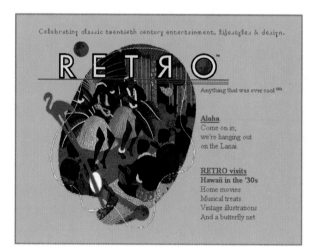

somber

Remembering Nagasaki—http://www.exploratorium.edu/nagasaki/

Black and white images, and white type on a black background, gives a suitable forum for a remembrance site such as this one. The black is somber and complementary to the images. If the background had been a bright color, the site wouldn't have maintained the proper mood, or may have seemed disrespectful to the occasion—much like wearing a brightly flowered shirt may be frowned upon at a traditional funeral.

cool/hip

Lumiére—http://www.lumiere.com/

If a site's personality could wear sunglasses, this one would. Even though the basic color scheme is the same neutral colors of black and white as in Remembering Nagasaki, here the attitude comes across as hip as a little black dress. Splashes of color in its images offer contrast, and direct the eye to the site's content.

funky/fun

BlenderWeb—http://www.blender.com/

Holy saturated colors, Batman! Um... remember that contrast stuff we were talking about? BlenderWeb is bright, high contrast, and painful to stare at for long periods of time, but also screams LOOK AT ME, DAMMIT! and you do. It's easy to see how choosing colors like this wouldn't work for a stock brokerage firm.

well–read

SALON—http://www.salon1999.com/

Light up a fine cigar, warm up the brandy, and lounge in front of your computer. SALON's color scheme gives it a simple yet sophisticated flavor, much like the New Yorker magazine.

137

we're big business but you can trust us 'cause we're people just like you

Bank of America—http://www.BankAmerica.com/

Now, my title for this category may have been biased by the happy faces that seem to beam out of this site, but the tone is also set by the clean-cut colors, as well. Again we see a red, white, and blue all-American palette: bright, hopeful, and confident. Would BofA's site have a different personality, if, say, they decided to use money-green as the basic hue of their palette?

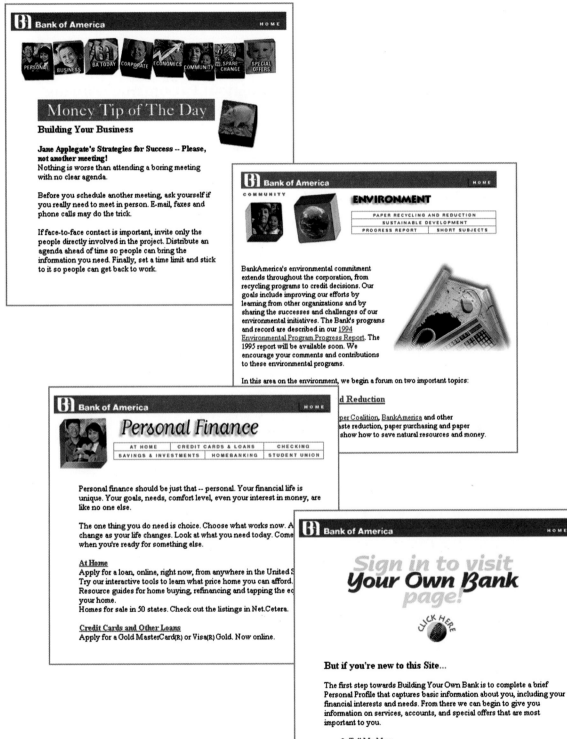

Bank of America HOME

PERSONAL BUSINESS BA TODAY CORPORATE ECONOMICS COMMUNITY SPARE CHANGE SPECIAL OFFERS

Money Tip of The Day

Building Your Business

Jane Applegate's Strategies for Success -- Please, not another meeting!
Nothing is worse than attending a boring meeting with no clear agenda.

Before you schedule another meeting, ask yourself if you really need to meet in person. E-mail, faxes and phone calls may do the trick.

If face-to-face contact is important, invite only the people directly involved in the project. Distribute an agenda ahead of time so people can bring the information you need. Finally, set a time limit and stick to it so people can get back to work.

Bank of America HOME

COMMUNITY

ENVIRONMENT

PAPER RECYCLING AND REDUCTION	
SUSTAINABLE DEVELOPMENT	
PROGRESS REPORT	SHORT SUBJECTS

BankAmerica's environmental commitment extends throughout the corporation, from recycling programs to credit decisions. Our goals include improving our efforts by learning from other organizations and by sharing the successes and challenges of our environmental initiatives. The Bank's programs and record are described in our 1994 Environmental Program Progress Report. The 1995 report will be available soon. We encourage your comments and contributions to these environmental programs.

In this area on the environment, we begin a forum on two important topics:

d Reduction

per Coalition, BankAmerica and other
aste reduction, paper purchasing and paper
show how to save natural resources and money.

Bank of America HOME

Personal Finance

AT HOME	CREDIT CARDS & LOANS	CHECKING
SAVINGS & INVESTMENTS	HOMEBANKING	STUDENT UNION

Personal finance should be just that -- personal. Your financial life is unique. Your goals, needs, comfort level, even your interest in money, are like no one else.

The one thing you do need is choice. Choose what works now. A change as your life changes. Look at what you need today. Come when you're ready for something else.

At Home
Apply for a loan, online, right now, from anywhere in the United S
Try our interactive tools to learn what price home you can afford.
Resource guides for home buying, refinancing and tapping the ec your home.
Homes for sale in 50 states. Check out the listings in Net.Cetera.

Credit Cards and Other Loans
Apply for a Gold MasterCard(R) or Visa(R) Gold. Now online.

Bank of America HOME

Sign in to visit
Your Own Bank
page!

CLICK HERE

But if you're new to this Site...

The first step towards Building Your Own Bank is to complete a brief Personal Profile that captures basic information about you, including your financial interests and needs. From there we can begin to give you information on services, accounts, and special offers that are most important to you.

- Tell Me More.
- Sounds Great! Sign me up.

CHAPTER 8

MOOD LIGHTING

earthy (with a tech twist)

Cyborganic Gardens—http://www.cyborganic.com/

Grassy green is the color prevalent throughout Cyborganic Gardens, and it works. They've combined grassy and forest greens, and other earthy colors (autumn golds and reds, bark brown, and so on), with touches of various shades of purple—perhaps to remind us that we're really in a virtual garden, not a real one.

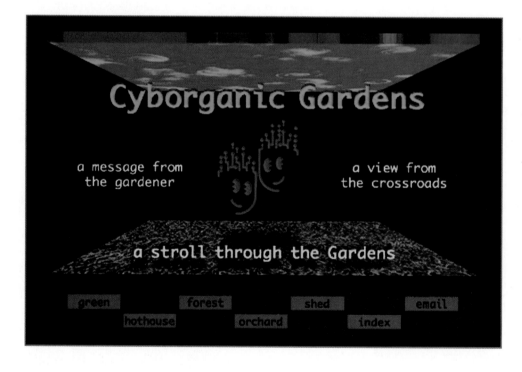

mysterious

The X-Files Official Web Site—http://www.thex-files.com/

ssshhh—someone might hear you... The neutral white-on-black works here to create mystery and intrigue; a ghostly effect that certainly emulates the show's theme. Nothing earthy about the green on this site; here we think "little green men" rather than cheerful springtime leaves of grass, as in Cyborganic Gardens.

THE (X) FILES

Case Files

This area contains deep background files about *The X-Files*

These files include an extensive episode guide complete with pictures from the episodes, downloadable items such as video promos, audio promos and advertisements, information about the show and its creator, cast biographies and photos, and thorough character biographies including pictures of your favorite -- and not-so-favorite -- characters

EPISODE GUIDE   SHOW INFORMATION   CHARACTER INFO

THE (X) FILES

Episode Guide

SEASON ONE

Title	Episode #	Air Date
Pilot	Pilot	09/10/93
DEEP THROAT	1X01	09/17/93
SQUEEZE	1X02	09/24/93
CONDUIT	1X03	10/01/93
THE JERSEY DEVIL	1X04	10/08/93
SHADOWS	1X05	10/22/93
GHOST IN THE MACHINE	1X06	10/29/93
ICE	1X07	11/05/93
SPACE	1X08	11/12/93
FALLEN ANGEL	1X09	11/19/93
EVE	1X10	12/10/93
FIRE	1X11	12/17/93
BEYOND THE SEA	1X12	01/07/94

MERCHANDISE

You are entering a Classified and Exclusive X-Files Merchandise Area. All items offered for sale in this area are currently available to the public only through The Official X-Files Web Site

Secure Area

Ground Zero Limited Collector's Edition

Ground Zero by Kevin J. Anderson

A secret nuclear project

A series of mysterious deaths

A planet in jeopardy

Autographed

Specially boxed

Numbered first edition

Item	Price	Enter Quantity
Novel	$49.95	

FORUM

The Official X-Files IRC Chat!

The X-Files official Web Site now has two IRC chat channels
These channels can be accessed with any IRC client and can be found on the server **chat.iguide.com**
The channels are:

#xfiles - The Official X-Files IRC Chat
#xpa - X-Philes Anonymous

The XPA, as you may know, is a fan club of sorts that meets tonight here on The Official X-Files Web Site and reached over 25 members in less than a month. For more info about how to become an established member check out the XPA topics in the Fan forum.

The Official X-Files Web Site Fan Forum

Click Here to access the forum

Please read the disclaimer below before accessing the new forum

Disclaimer

This is intended to be a forum for discussion of "THE X-FILES" in particular and for the discussion of the paranormal in general. Anything appearing on this forum regarding "THE X-FILES" is not considered confidential information and is the property of Twentieth Century Fox Film Corporation ("Fox"). The posting of any material regarding "THE X-FILES" section of this forum constitutes an unlimited assignment of such material to Fox. In order to have "THE X-FILES" producers participate, you must comply with the foregoing assignment. Thanks for your cooperation.

summary

You don't have to be a color theorist to see that certain colors can mean certain things, and combinations of colors, or variations in color hues and value, can make a big difference in how a site's image comes across. While there are no rules to follow when choosing colors for a site, there are logical choices to create a combination of uniqueness, creativity, and readability.

TIP: COLOR THEORY

If color theory fascinates you, the following are helpful sites that discuss the artistic and/or psychological effects of color:

Color Theory
http://www.contrib.andrew.cmu.edu:8001/usr/dw4e/color/color.html

Reviews of Color Theory Resources
http://www.prairienet.org/quilts/theory.html

Gary's Guide to Graphics: Color Theory
http://www.cs.gmu.edu:80/~garyq/graphics_guide/color_theory/

Basic Color Theory
http://www.coa.edu/HEJourney/polcom/colort.html

Interaction Design – color theory
http://www.user.com/color.htm

ColorTheoryIndex.html
http://www.macproa.com/ColorTheoryIndex.html

JVS DESIGN COLOR THEORY-MENU
http://www.bway.net/~jscruggs/color.html

type & style

make your words speak out

"When ideas fail, words come in very handy."

— Goethe

145

Before the web became famous for its ability to bring us graphics and animation and sound effects, it brought us text. Sure, it wasn't just any old regular text; it was *hyper*text. But still, text is text, and it certainly has benefited from the addition of the other elements mentioned.

Yet text is still the most crucial form of communication medium on the web, even if it's imbedded in an image map or serving as an explanation in an ALT tag. The issue we've got to face with text on the web is the same no matter how we present it: **readability**. Read it or weep.

it's default's fault

The default proportional typeface that we are used to seeing on the web, and what happens to be the default font for most browsers, is Times Roman. For Netscape Navigator, its default size is 12 point. For Microsoft's Internet Explorer; its default size is "medium," or 14 points. The default monospace typeface tends to be Courier 12 point, and default monospace type in forms or input boxes tends to be 10 point Courier. So far, you have a whole two typefaces to choose from. Are you excited yet?

The thing is, if a person on the other end of your web site (the viewer) has changed any of his or her default type faces or sizes, chances are your site is going to look significantly different. When you design something for print, it comes out of the printer looking a certain way, and you know exactly what it is your readers are getting.

If the viewer changes their default browser typeface, even a simple page like this one will look like... well, for lack of a better word, poo.

There's no real getting around this except for hoping loudly that people don't change their default typeface (and I know few who do, except to possibly make the default size slightly bigger), or putting a notice on your site that says "this site looks best when viewed with 12-point Times Roman as your proportional typeface, and 12-point Courier as your monospace typeface." There are those visitors, however, who don't like being told what to do and just may view your site in Script just to see how funny they can make it look. I may be one of them.

rules about reading

It's generally agreed that 60 characters per line (or fewer) is simply easier to read than longer lines. This is because when you're done with one line, your eyes don't have to "search" for the beginning of the next line because it's close enough to the end of the last one. To test yourself, take any page of text, change your page setup to landscape, make text a standard 10 or 12 point, print it out, and notice it's more of a pain to read.

As you can see, when type is small and it doesn't break here, after about 60 characters, it's much more difficult to read. It's even harder to read if the type is this small! Imagine how tired your readers will get if they had to read page after page of type that spread far, far across pages without any place for their eyes to rest. It's more difficult for our eyes to find the beginning of the next sentence if text spreads too far without breaking, as well.

If text is layed out in one long long line, your eyes have no place to stop, and it's easy to lose your place if you happen to look away. It's sort of like if we didn't have punctuation or capital letters at the beginning of sentences we would never stop reading or know when to pause we end up spending more time trying to figure out when to stop than reading and enjoying ourselves if you know what i mean and i think you do by now

Basically, our eyes (and our brains) need guidance.

CHAPTER 9

TYPE

147

column conundrum

In one sense, columns make text easier to read, even though our eyes have to jump from the bottom of a column to the top of the next column. We've become used to having to jump around from one column to another in order to continue reading a story—but it's important to make sure that columns are not too close together or too far apart. It's also helpful if columns aren't too short or too long and if the tops of the columns are aligned if possible, or readers will have to work more in order to find their way around. On the printed page, this may not be as crucial because the page has a limited amount of space to fill up, and the viewer can usually see the whole page at once. Therefore, they can see the top of the next column from the bottom of the previous column long before they have to jump their eyes up there.

This is an example of text in columns. Note how your eye has to jump from the bottom of this column to the top of the next column. This isn't so bad; we've kinda gotten used to having to jump around from one column to another in order to continue reading a story.

But it's important to make sure that columns are not too close together, or too far apart. It is also helpful if columns aren't too short or too long, or the reader will have to "work" more in order to find their way around.

On the printed page, this may not be as crucial, because the page has a limited amount of space, and the viewer can see the whole page at once. Therefore, they can see the top of the next column from the bottom of the previous column long before they have to jump their eyes up there.

On a web page, if a person is forced to scroll

In this example, the text columns have been set too wide apart. Notice how it's more difficult to find the top of the next column from the bottom of the previous column.

Here, the columns are much too close together. So close, that it's difficult to even discern between them. The reader's eyes may try to read straight across the page instead of down the column.

This is an example of text in columns. Note how your eye has to jump from the bottom of this column to the top of the next column. This isn't so bad; we've kinda gotten used to having to jump around from one column to another in order to continue reading a story.

But it's important to make sure that columns are not too close together, or too far apart. It is also helpful if columns aren't too short or too long, or the reader will have to "work" more in order to find their way around.

On a web page, if a person is forced to scroll down a long way to read one column and then have to scroll back up the page to jump to the next, it's easier for them to get lost.

This is an example of text in columns. Note how your eye has to jump from the bottom of this column to the top of the next column. This isn't so bad; we've kinda gotten used to having to jump around from one column to another in order to continue reading a story.

But it's important to make sure that columns are not too close together, or too far apart. It is also helpful if columns aren't too short or too long, or the reader will have to "work" more in order to find their way around.

On the printed page, this may not be as crucial, because the page has a limited amount of space, and the viewer can see the whole page at once. Therefore, they can see the top of the next column from the bottom of the previous column long before they have to jump their eyes up there.

On a web page, if a person is forced to scroll down a long way to read one column and then have to scroll back up the page to jump to the next, it's easier for them to get lost.

Here, there's sufficient space between columns, but not too much. It's pretty easy to figure out where to go from the bottom of each column.

Even if your columns are spaced nicely on a web page, however, if you force your viewers to scroll down a long way to read one column and then have to scroll back up the page to jump to the next column, their chances of getting lost are much higher. Think of when you've tried reading a full-sized newspaper on the subway train, or in a small space so that you've had to fold your paper in order not to give your neighbor a paper cut—you get to the end of a column, then you have to unfold the paper, search for the next column, and hopefully find it if you unfold the paper in the most logical way. If you table your text in columns, keep them as short as possible.

less work, more reading

What it all comes down to is that any time our eyes have to do more work, the less easy it is to read. Take a read through the following paragraphs, and as you read, take note of how your eyes are moving and/or stammering through the words:

IT'S MORE WORK TO READ LARGE BODIES OF TEXT IN ALL CAPS BECAUSE IT'S HARDER FOR OUR EYES TO DIFFERENTIATE AMONG THE LETTERS. LOOKING AT A LARGE AMOUNT OF ALL CAPS TEXT ALSO MAKES THE WHOLE PARAGRAPH OR PAGE BLEND INTO A VISUAL BLOB. AFTER A WHILE THE WHOLE SET OF WORDS KIND OF WHIRLS INTO A BLUR OF MEANINGLESS MARKINGS. THERE'S NOTHING TO STOP OR CATCH OUR EYE.

It's pretty
difficult to read a large body of
centered text—especially if the
lines are of significantly different sizes—because,
again, the reader's eye has
to go searching for the beginning of the next line.
Each line starts in a different
place, and
it's more work for a person's eyes to find the
beginning of the line following the one they
just finished reading.

CHAPTER 9 TYPE

149

Text that is aligned on the right
is also harder to read than text that is aligned on the
left, for the same reason as when
something is centered.

Columns are helpful to make reading easier, but if
they
are too
thin, or
if there
are man–
y hyphen–
ated
words,
it puts
too many
"pauses"
in the
sentence, again obstructing reading ease. Not to mention that it looks
kinda icky.

digestible portions

While we may not be able to control exactly what a person is seeing, we can still help them along in the readability department by breaking up our text content into comfortable chunks.

To ensure comfortable reading, break up long passages of text into paragraphs, just like this book and so many other books have been broken up. You can do this quite simply by adding the <P> tag, which throws a line space between paragraphs.

Another visual aide is the subhead. You may have noticed them throughout this book—the words "digestible portions" are a subhead for this section of this chapter. A key to creating a useful subhead is to make its type size large enough to be well discernible from the body text, so that it stands out from the main text. A subhead that is the same size, or too similar in size, will simply fade away into the mass of text on the page. That's why the subheads in this book are significantly different than the body type (but not so big as to distract you completely from the body text)—it shows you, the reader, that "hey! here's a new section!" as well as giving your eyes a place to rest and differentiate this section from other sections.

Subhead Success
This is an example of a satisfactory subhead that works in relation to the following text because it's proportionally larger enough to easily distinguish it from the body text. This body text is 12 points Times Roman, the default size of text in most browsers. The subhead, in web-speak, would be tagged with <H3></H3> surrounding it—resulting in a 14 point bold Times Roman subhead.

graphical text

One of the beauties of graphical web browsers is that we can substitute bland text with graphics of text. If we create a stylish text logo, or want to use a specific typeface for headlines, subheads, or even all of the body type, we can use our graphics applications to create GIFs or JPEGs to fill in for our Times Roman friend. My site's logo is mostly made out of text, but I threw it in Photoshop, stuck a gausian blur behind it, and presto, I have a GIF that is more visually stimulating than the bold Times Roman type that would result if I had simply used a headline tag, such as <H1></H1>.

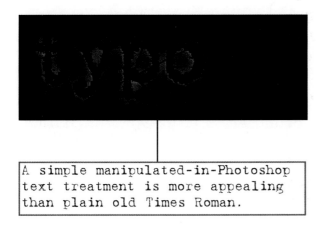

A simple manipulated-in-Photoshop text treatment is more appealing than plain old Times Roman.

RETRO's main menu wouldn't portray its image nearly as effectively if it had chosen to use non-graphical text for its section titles. (http://www.retroactive.com/)

double-spacing

suck.com, the folks with the fish, a barrel, and a smoking gun, use a couple of tricks to give it its trademark text layout. First of all, the column is set in a narrow table, and all the text within the table is centered. While I said previously that large blocks of centered text is harder to read than text that is all aligned on the left, suck does a pretty good job of breaking its lines so that they are all very close to being the same length.

Over at suck, (http://www.suck.com/), its characteristic look is created by centering the text within a table; it's double-spaced using paragraph break tags after each line.

There's no code yet to automatically double-space text, so to achieve the effect on its page, each line has a paragraph break <P> that puts a line space in between each line. The Black Box web site (http://www.ot.com/black-box/home.html) uses <P> tags to create the impression of double-spaced text, as well. Some sites insert a transparent GIF spacer within each line to control the distance between text lines. This gives you more control over the vertical line spacing (also known as "leading"), but if someone visits your site with images turned off; they'll be seeing lots of [IMAGE] fillers or the empty-graphic icons in every line.

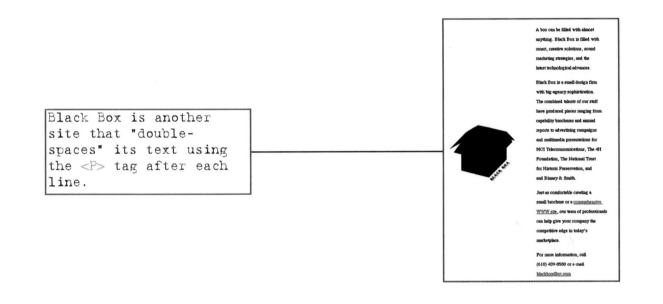

```
Black Box is another
site that "double-
spaces" its text using
the <P> tag after each
line.
```

blockquote

Another common tag used to format text to make it more readable—by adding margin space on either side of text (and usually a line of space above and below text)—is BLOCKQUOTE. The BLOCKQUOTE tag around text usually indents text about an inch from both the left and right margins. However, some browsers read the BLOCKQUOTE tag as a cue to italicize text. So unless you know that most of your viewers are using a browser that will indent rather than italicize this tag, use it with caution on big blocks of text—lots of italic type is also difficult to read on screen.

153

The NWHQ site (http://www.knosso.com/NWHQ/) uses the BLOCK-QUOTE tag to indent introductory text on its initial page. This enhances the text's readability, especially since the viewer has to widen the default browser window to fit the entire design of the opening image/text, above. And while we're speaking of interesting text effects, note the site's intriguing use of text and links surrounding the central image map.

Most other tags, such as lists and font attribution tags, can be used within the BLOCK-QUOTE tag for added flexibility.

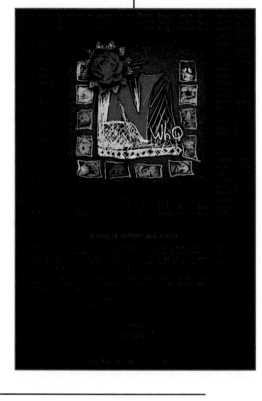

pre, tt, & code mode

If Times Roman is boring you to tears, there's always Courier to turn to. While Courier is far from being dashing, its simple form seems to have made a comeback in the web design world. It's like going back to the days of pre–PostScript printers.

I used the PRE tag on my menu page to give me control of where spaces and letters fell in this pattern. On most other pages where I use Courier as my body text, I use the CODE tag.

Courier is monospaced, which means each character—no matter if it's a skinny "l" or a wide "m"—take up the same amount of space. Capital letters and lower case letters also take up the same amount of space. Like Times Roman, Courier sports serifs, or those little lines that jut off the edges of the letters. Serif typefaces are generally used as body copy, while headlines and subheads are generally san serif, or without serifs, like Helvetica.

`This is Courier. All letters are the same width.`

This is Times Roman. It's a proportional typeface with serifs.

Helvetica, as you can see, has no serifs.

Many sites now use the PRE (preformatted), TT (teletype), and CODE tags to give their body text the typewriter treatment, including yours truly.

```
The biography section of the Haring.com
site (http://www.haring.com/
keith/bio/bio.html) uses the <TT> tag
for its site. Note, though, that font
attribution tags, such as FONT SIZE, are
still recognized (I really like how the
site designer uses the contrast in type
size to set off the comments from the
actual biography text). The entire page,
by the way, is indented on both the left
and right using BLOCKQUOTE.
```

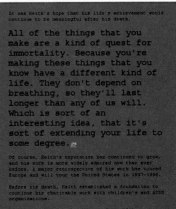

MetaDesign (http://www.
metadesign.com/) utilizes
the TT, or teletype style
tag, to Courierize its site.
Note how they set it off
with a contrasting graphic
pull-quote and headline
text.

The main difference among these tags is that the PRE code follows the format of exactly what you type, such as spaces and hard returns, while TT and CODE tend to follow—or need to follow—basic HTML directions, and will automatically wrap, follow size attributions, and so on.

color & contrast

There's no doubt at all that high contrast between text and its background is a key element in its readability. If you can't see it, you can't read it. If you can't read it, your visitors can't read it either. Take a look through your book shelves and you'll notice that most of your books probably use black ink on white or very light ivory colored paper.

Since the light flying out of your monitor may make large amounts of white too eye-strainful to stare at for long periods of time, you might like to try setting your text color a little lighter than black—maybe hex value #333333 (RGB values: 051–051–051). Similarly, if you choose to use a dark background for your page, you have to have contrasting text. You don't need to use black and white as your text and background colors to make your site readable. You just need to make sure there's significant enough contrast between the two colors.

a note on background tiles and contrast

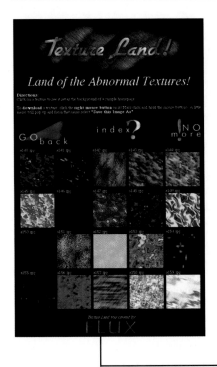

Texture Land! from FLUX (http://www.meat.com/textures/) offers hundreds of images for use for free on non–commercial web sites (write them for details if you want to use them on a commercial site). While some of them are eye-dazzling, and it's tempting to use them as is, it's rare to find a background pattern saturated with bright colors that's easy to place text over—and have it remain readable.

A handy source for wild background textures is Texture Land!, from the same team that brings us The Enhanced for Netscape Hall of Shame.

Here's one of Texture Land's images made into a background tile. No matter what color or size text I use, I can't get consistent readability, because there's not enough overall contrast.

157

If I darken or lighten the image - or reduce the contrast among the colors in the tile - it's still not perfect, but readability is enhanced tremendously.

Now I can read light text on this background - if it is big enough. **Don't you agree?**

Now I can read dark text on this background - if it is big enough. **If the text is bold, it's even easier to read on a textured background.**

Whether you use any of these textures or create background tiles of your own, make sure you can actually read the text you put over them. Even if one or two words are unreadable, it affects your site's image.

TIP: TYPOGRAPHY 101

For an overview of typography, letter forms, and how different text effects affect readability and design, click over to typoGRAPHIC

(http://www.razorfish.com/bluedot/typo/). Not only is the site lovely to look at, there are interactive pages in which you can determine the size and spacing of type to view how your changes affect the way type looks and works. Be prepared with a Shockwavable browser to take advantage of some of the type activities.

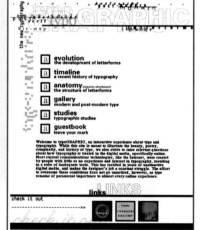

summary

I'll bet that text will always be a major form of communication and information exchange on the web, even if it's incorporated into images or all sites become animated, sound-appended multimedia masterpieces.

Enhancing and ensuring text readability is key to making your site a pleasant place to peruse. Check to make sure—especially if you use background tiles—that text is large enough, that it contrasts with your background, and that its spacing enhances layout and clarity. Use subheads and graphical elements to break up large gobs of text. I'll say it again: if you can't read your stuff, neither can your viewers, so lighten up your backgrounds, darken your text, or do whatever you can to enhance contrast.

CHAPTER 9

TYPE

graphic appeal

basic rules for web graphics

"Whoever controls the media—the images—controls the culture."

— Allen Ginsberg

It's rare to find a web page that doesn't use graphics as visual elements on its pages. It's one of the reasons that the web is a cool place to explore, and also what makes the web frustrating at times. A picture really can be worth a thousand words—but on the web, a picture's only worth a thousand words if it's only a few thousand bytes and we don't have to wait a thousand years for it to appear on our screen. There's a number of things you can do to keep images as unobtrusive as possible, and increase their value to your audience. Images should be used to enhance your content, not take it over—even if your site is an art gallery.

The key element to creating good graphics is to make images small. When I say make your images small, I don't mean make them only an inch high or less. What I really mean is to passionately suck as many kilobytes out of them in as many ways as you can. Many of the methods to do so are in the following guidelines.

good graphic guidelines

check your colors

If you haven't heard of the 216-color browser-safe palette yet, get over to http://www.lynda.com/hex.html and download one or both of the color palettes that are available there (one is arranged by hue; one by value). Open up the palette in the art program of your choice, and use the eye-dropper tool to select the browser-safe colors as you need them.

As mentioned in the Mood Lighting chapter (beginning on page 110), browser-safe colors are guaranteed not to dither on screen. Dithering, or spotty, rough colors, is what happens when a color is not available in the browser's palette, and the browser tries to compensate by combining pixels of other colors to make up for the missing color, possibly making colors look splotchy and uneven. When your image is strewn with dithers, significant and unnecessary kilobytes are added to the file.

Your image may look great in Photoshop or other graphics programs, but check them in whatever browser you're using before you put them on your site. In most browsers that will view GIFs or JPEGs, for example, you can go to your File menu, and chose "open local file" or "open file" to view a GIF or JPEG that's on your hard drive.

use the right graphic format

GIF (formally known as Graphics Interchange Format) is a type of image compression file format that has been used to make bitmapped images smaller for efficient online transfer and viewing for many years. Its compression scheme is effective, especially in images that use a lot of flat colors (which means images that aren't photographs or that have a lot of dithering), because it bases its compression on the number of times pixel colors change along the horizontal axis of an image. The more colors, the bigger the GIF. However, because GIFs are indexed images, it means that they can hold no more than 256 colors, which is why they aren't the best format for photographs or images that originally have more than 256 colors.

GIFs come in two different flavors—GIF87a and GIF89a—and the tiniest of them is GIF89a. When you save an indexed image as a CompuServe GIF (which is one of the file formats in Photoshop and other popular graphics applications), you're saving it as a GIF87a. To save it as a GIF89a, which is necessary if you want to make your image transparent or interlaced, you'll need an application that will either translate your image, or a plug-in for your graphics application that will save as GIF89a.

Transparent GIFs can be cool because when done properly, it gives the appearance of an irregularly shaped image on your page's background. This can be preferable to the typical rectangular blockiness of an image against a background, depending on the image and background. Here are some examples:

Here's my original GIF image.

163

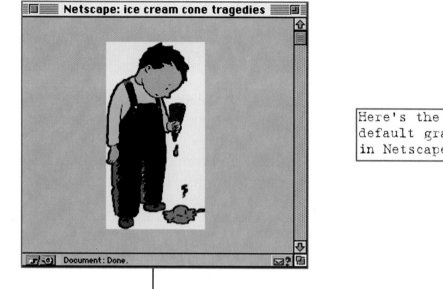

Here's the image on the default gray background in Netscape Navigator.

This time I simply changed the BG COLOR to equal the same shade as the yellow surrounding the boy. In this case, it's not really necessary to save the boy with the yellow as the transparent color, since it seems to be transparent if the background is the same color.

If I add a background tile, even if its main color is the same as the image's background color, there's an image edge that cuts into the background image. This edge would be even more apparent if the background's main color were just a little bit off.

Once I make the background color of the boy transparent, however, it now sits peacefully atop the background.

Interlaced GIFs appear on the screen as a whole, in lower resolution blocks that rev up to full resolution as the file loads. While this may be preferable to watching a GIF draw downward from the top to the bottom of the image as it loads, some designers think the effect is ugly when interlaced images do their chunky thing. It does, however, help viewers determine more quickly whether or not they're in the right place, or want to stay and wait for the rest of the image to download. By the way, interlaced images don't load any faster than their regular counterparts.

JPEGs are generally best used on images with lots of subtle changes in colors, such as photographs. Its compression method is "lossy" —it cuts out colors and approximates them with colors that are within the palette. The good thing about JPEGs is that you can save images in 24–bit, and when they are decompressed on someone's screen who happens to have their monitor set to that resolution, they'll be able to appreciate the greater resolution.

A JPEG can save even more space in an image file than a GIF, but can take more time to decompress. So if your image file is about the same size when saved in JPEG or GIF (and it looks OK as a GIF), then those people with slower modems will be able to view the GIF image a bit more quickly.

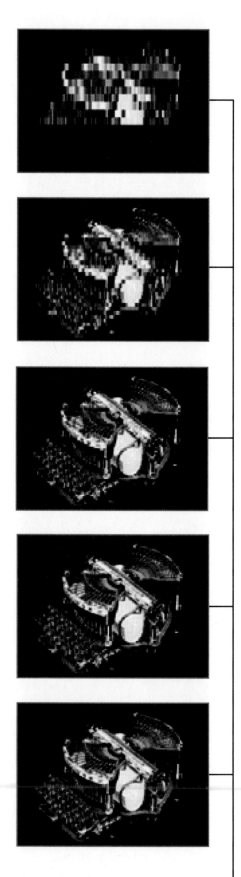

This procession of images shows how an interlaced GIF draws itself in ever-increasing-resolution blocks, rather than drawing down one line of the image at a time.

TIP: PROGRESSIVE JPEGs

Progressive JPEG is a compression scheme that loads JPEGs into your browser in a similar way an interlaced GIF is loaded, which will cut down image loading time overall. Most common browsers now support Progressive JPEGs, and there are a number of utilities available to help create them.

crop photos

Unless you're right-on with every photograph you take, chances are there's some of it that you can crop, or cut off the edges, in order to make it a more potent image. Here are two examples: one taken with an Apple QuickTake camera, and one with a Connectix QuickCam.

The original photo of Internet the cat is 144 dpi, and has a lot of extraneous floor around him, which detracts from the point of the picture: to show the cat. At this point, the image is a 900K RGB file; as a JPEG, it stands at 24K.

Here, I cropped out all of the image that's not relevant, cut the dpi to 72, and the image now is a tiny 3K JPEG.

This photo was captured with a Connectix QuickCam at 72 dpi. As a JPEG, it's only 15K. But unless the point in this image is to show Carla's height compared to the door and whiteboard behind her (which, due to the camera, look severely out of proportion), it will serve the photo well to be cropped.

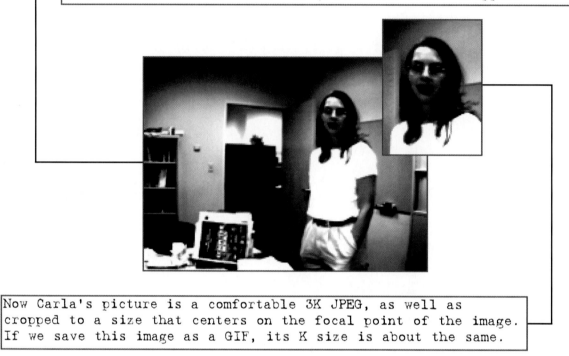

Now Carla's picture is a comfortable 3K JPEG, as well as cropped to a size that centers on the focal point of the image. If we save this image as a GIF, its K size is about the same.

save images as 72 dpi

If you use a digital camera or scanner to bring your artwork or photos into your computer, or are using artwork that has appeared in print, one of the easiest ways to cut down significantly on file size is to change its resolution to 72 dots per inch. While you may think that saving an image at a higher resolution may make an image look better (and it does on paper), it isn't so for the web, since computer monitors show us stuff at a whopping 72 dpi, and that's it.

Here's an example of how the dpi of an image determine it's byte size. Each one of these images is one inch tall by one inch wide, and would look the same when viewed at this size on a 72 dpi screen. And yet the resolution of the image decreases significantly, even from a relatively low-resolution scan of 150 dpi. Let's compare the same image at different resolutions that are saved as GIF89a.

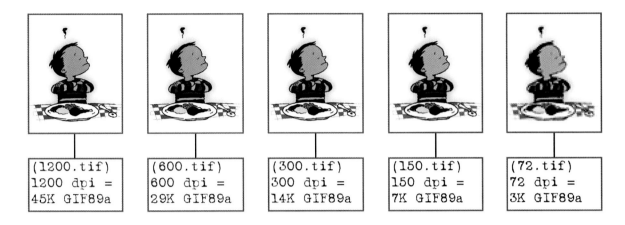

(1200.tif)	(600.tif)	(300.tif)	(150.tif)	(72.tif)
1200 dpi =	600 dpi =	300 dpi =	150 dpi =	72 dpi =
45K GIF89a	29K GIF89a	14K GIF89a	7K GIF89a	3K GIF89a

Just in case you're thinking, "Hey, 45K isn't so big; why should I go to the trouble of fixing that?," I'd like you to remember that this is an itsy bitsy one-inch image—chances are there will be more than this on your page, and even itsy bitsy images add up very quickly.

Keep in mind that if you're going to be manipulating an image, working with a larger file is OK. It almost always looks better to shrink down an image than to resize up.

don't resize images in index mode

One common mistake on sites is images that have been resized *after* they've been converted to GIFs, or while in Indexed mode. If you're going to resize images, make sure you've changed to RGB mode in order to avoid giving your images the "jaggies."

Here's my original 72 dpi GIF that I want to resize.

If I resize the cowboy kid in indexed mode, its edges are jaggy - whether I make it smaller or bigger.

If I change the image to RGB and then resize (and then save again as a GIF), the image's edges remain smooth.

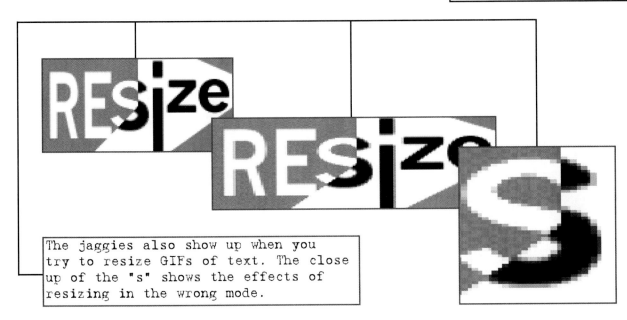

The jaggies also show up when you try to resize GIFs of text. The close up of the "s" shows the effects of resizing in the wrong mode.

use thumbnails

One way to cut down on people's art annoyance is to present them with a menu of thumbnails to view larger representations of the images. This is a good method for high-graphic sites such as galleries or photo albums.

In my site's gallery and other areas where there are choices of many images to view, I generally create thumbnails of each image and let the viewer know how big the larger image is - in this case, the K sizes are below each respective image. Viewers can then decide whether or not they want to continue on. Note that I've given them a line of directions - click on a thumbnail below to view a larger image" - just in case they haven't encountered this kind of layout before.

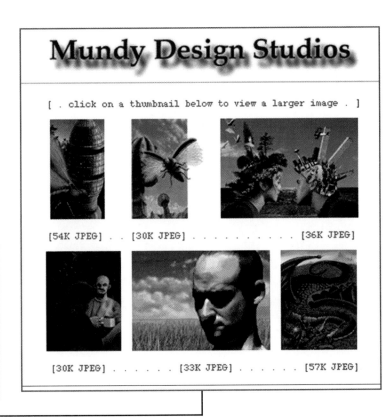

CHAPTER 10

GRAPHICS

171

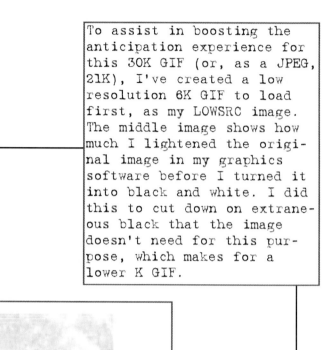

To assist in boosting the anticipation experience for this 30K GIF (or, as a JPEG, 21K), I've created a low resolution 6K GIF to load first, as my LOWSRC image. The middle image shows how much I lightened the original image in my graphics software before I turned it into black and white. I did this to cut down on extraneous black that the image doesn't need for this purpose, which makes for a lower K GIF.

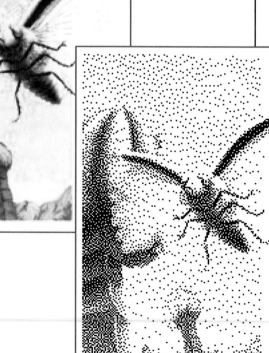

specify your image size

By specifying the image height and width in your tag, browsers such as Netscape will keep "place holders" of those images while the rest of the page loads. To add the height and width attributes of an image, use the following:

<IMG SRC="sam.gif" WIDTH=215 HEIGHT=285>

The numbers refer to the size of the image in pixels. If you're not sure of an image's size, open it up in your graphics application and change your unit of measurement to pixels. If you have Netscape Navigator, open up the image file. Choose Open File from the File menu. Mac people, hold down your mouse button on the image and choose View this Image. Windows people, click on the image with the right mouse button and choose View this Image. When the image comes up in Navigator, its dimensions will appear in the title bar, height by width in pixels.

TIP: FINDING GRAPHICS RESOURCES

A search for "progressive JPEG" or "transparent GIF" in Yahoo (http://www.yahoo.com/) should bring up updated links to those companies that offer plug-ins and translators. Or drop into shareware.com (http://www.shareware.com/) and do a search under your specific platform.

summary

You don't need to sacrifice an image's quality or impact to a page if you prepare an image the right way in the first place. If you keep image size down, crop images appropriately, save using the correct format, and insert appropriate tags and comments, your images will look better, and your site will be enhanced by graphics instead of hindered.

gizmos, gadgets, & gif animations

are they amazing or annoying?

"Power corrupts. Absolute power is kind of neat."

— John Lehman (Secretary of the US Navy 1981-1987)

175

In this chapter, we'll take a look at some of the gizmos and gadgets to have hit the web, see how they've been implemented, and try to determine when it is and is not appropriate to take advantage (or invest time and money in) these "new" technologies.

Everywhere there's stuff said about the web, you're bound to see or hear discussion of Java, Shockwave, and other nifty new toys to make the web experience more exciting and interactive. Java is so hot that (according to the grapevine), by the end of 1996, there will be over 150 books published on this language alone. Are you thinking you should run out and learn Java? Or maybe Director and Lingo? Well, before you do, determine whether their effects will be amazing or annoying to those viewing your site.

According to the GVU's WWW Surveying Team's latest results in its fifth web survey which ended in April 1996, in which users were asked to rate on a scale of 1 to 9 how much they liked pages which contained images, meta-indexes (such as Lycos or Yahoo), movies, sounds, search engines, and text, the average was a not-so-whopping 5 for images. Just images! no motion or sound to speak of. Interestingly, the rating was lower for text, at 4.5, then sound at 4.2, and movies (including animations) topped off at 3.9. Users like sites that were searchable (7.6) or were meta-indices (7.5)—sites that helped them find the information they were looking for.[1]

who are you trying to impress?

Tired of seeing these in your browser window? So am I. Some plug-ins may look cool, but are they really necessary?

Here's the thing: I believe that too many web designers are jumping on the gizmo bandwagon just because they know how to. Web sites become web designer's and programmer's portfolio pieces instead of sites developed with their users in mind. Most people don't have the speed, the time, the

[1]GVU's WWW Surveying Team's Fifth web survey. Graphics, Visualization, & Usability Center, College of Computing, Georgia Institute of Technology: http://www.cc.gatech.edu/gvu/user_surveys/.

browser, the plug–ins, or the patience to wait around for an applet to execute, or a GIF animation to fulfill its loop when they'd rather be accessing the information that a site holds. Again, according to the GVU's WWW Surveying Team's results, 25.5 percent of people accessing the web are still using 14.4 modems (just so you know, 39.0 percent use 28.8 modems).

Here's another thing that I don't think us big–wig city–dwelling ISDN and T1–enhanced designers and writers think about enough: there are still many areas in the U.S. (and I'm sure in other countries, too) where local–access dial–up does not exist, either from local providers or the big online services, so people are spending at least seven cents a minute on a 14.4 waiting for pages to load. Of course, depending on your goals for your site and your target audience, this may be of little consequence in your site design.

I've got to disclaim a bit here: I'm not saying that it's not a good thing to take advantage of these technologies. I'm not saying that as designers, we shouldn't push the limits of a browser. I'm just asking that we humble ourselves a bit, and keep the "paying customer"—those people spending at least twenty bucks a month accessing the 'net—in view. Just for fun, dig out the old 14.4 and sign on to the web. See what a lot of the world is missing. Keep making your Shockwave applications and compiling JavaScripts—just make sure you're doing it for a reason, and not just for your resume.

End another lecture. For now.

java

To find out more about the Java programming language, go straight to the source. JavaSoft's site is found at http://java.sun.com/.

According to Sun Microsystems' branch JavaSoft (the perpetrators of the Java programming language), "Java is a simple, robust, object–oriented, platform–independent multi–threaded, dynamic general–purpose programming environment. It's best for creating applets and applications for the Internet, intranets and any other complex, distributed network." Whew!

The key word you'll see floating about is "applets." An applet is a cute name for a miniature application that will run within a browser's page, such as a game (Tic Tac Toe example—http://java.sun.com/applets/applets/TicTacToe/example1.html), an animation (Bubbles example—http://java.sun.com/applets/applets/Bubbles/index.html), or more meaty usage, such as an appointment book (http://www.bookstore.com/main.html), if you so wished to keep your schedule webified.

To view applets on the web, viewers need a browser that supports them: at the time of this writing, Sun's browser, HotJava (still in beta), and Netscape Navigator support applets. They will soon to be supported by Microsoft's Internet Explorer (http://www.microsoft.com/) and Oracle's PowerBrowser (http://www.oracle.com/).

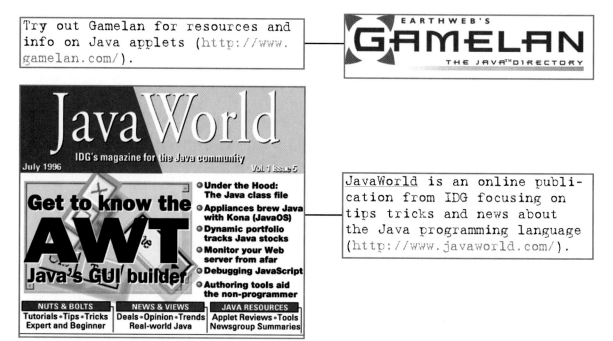

Try out Gamelan for resources and info on Java applets (http://www.gamelan.com/).

JavaWorld is an online publication from IDG focusing on tips tricks and news about the Java programming language (http://www.javaworld.com/).

the amazing factor: Being able to increase your site's value with a Java–enhanced, interactive application rather than offering plain old static text or simple forms.

the annoying factor: Only a few browsers now support Java, and since it's a programming language, you'll either have to learn programming or purchase an "instant" visual Java programming application, such as Hyperwire from Kinetix, a division of AutoDesk (http://www.ktx.com/).

javascript

JavaScripts are often confused with Java, the programming language. JavaScript is what the name implies: a scripting language—which basically means that you can create effects, such as scrolling text in the bottom status bar, or make a browser (that supports JavaScript) resize to the width and height you want—but you can't create applications, like you can with Java or other programming languages.

The coolest thing about JavaScripts is that you can often go to a site that features a JavaScript, and even if you have no experience programming, you can view the source, and cut and paste stuff from the script to suit your own tastes. (Many JavaScript authors, by the way, say this is fine with them, as long as you give them credit somehow, or don't alter the comments tags within the code. Be sure to check with each author about their usage terms before you go on a free-for-all JavaScript copying jaunt—and abide by their terms.)

So what can you do with JavaScript? Sure, you can post the date and the time on your site, or produce a scrolling message that says "Welcome to blah blah site!"—but how exciting is that?

The JavaScript Index, by Andrew Lee Woodridge, hosts samples, resources, and everything else you'd ever want to know about the art. (http://www.c2.org/~andreww/javascript/)

An interesting—and potentially widespread and practical—application of JavaScript is shown at HomePages, Inc. (http://www.homepages.com/fun/1040EZ.html). Just for fun, fill out a 1040EZ form to see how much tax you owe. Wouldn't it be cool if the IRS adopted a web-based filing system like this? Maybe more of us would file on time.

HomePages Inc. has created a JavaScript enhanced 1040EZ form that shows the future potential practical possibilities with this kind of technology. The form gives instantaneous feedback on entered numbers.

Another interesting—but not totally practical—application is showcased within "The Temple of Bel'Hargül" game by CyberDungeon (http://www.cyberdungeon.com/game/game.html).

Its use of JavaScript lets the game player receive hints about the game, use "magic," pick up items, and navigate through the scenery. It's a good example of JavaScript used for a reason, even if you're not into gaming.

the amazing factor: JavaScripts are relatively easy for non-programmers to customize for their own use, especially if the author puts instructions in comments fields or in read-me files.

the annoyance factor: Because JavaScripts are cut-and-paste-able, too many sites use its effects (such as scrolling messages in an on-screen

The Temple of Bel'Hargul, an interactive web game by CyberDungeon, takes advantage of JavaScript to make its interactive adventure... well, interactive.

window or along the bottom of your browser status bar) for no apparent use but to show that they have them. A status bar message that scrolls across too fast is annoying—plus it writes over any of the status information (such as a link's URL) that is useful for navigational purposes. Not to mention that some JavaScripts love to bomb the browser.

shockwave

If you're familiar with Macromedia's Authorware, Director, and FreeHand applications, you're basically armed to create what the company bills as Shockwave "Active Objects." Active objects include animations, sounds, and scalable and "zoomable" art. Once you've created a piece using one of the Macromedia's mentioned products, you then compress it using (yes, the same company's) compression utility, Afterburner.

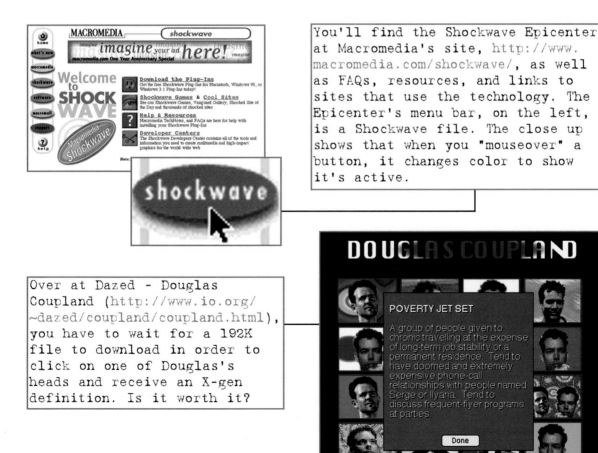

You'll find the Shockwave Epicenter at Macromedia's site, http://www.macromedia.com/shockwave/, as well as FAQs, resources, and links to sites that use the technology. The Epicenter's menu bar, on the left, is a Shockwave file. The close up shows that when you "mouseover" a button, it changes color to show it's active.

Over at Dazed - Douglas Coupland (http://www.io.org/~dazed/coupland/coupland.html), you have to wait for a 192K file to download in order to click on one of Douglas's heads and receive an X-gen definition. Is it worth it?

181

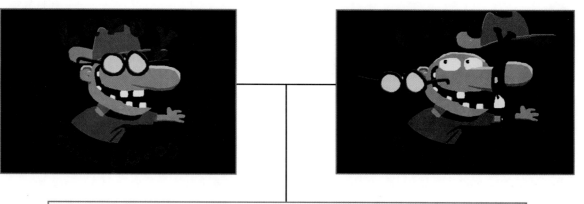

This 12K Shockwave file was created in Macromedia Director by Bruce Heavin. Find Leroy at http://home.earthlink.net/ ~bruceheavin/leroy.html and dismember him yourself.

the amazing factor: Being able to embed interactive applications and features that are fun to use or practical and have "instantaneous" feedback—meaning if you move something on the screen with your cursor, it moves.

the annoyance factor: It's another plug-in/feature to worry about your viewers having—or not having. Viewers still have to wait for files to download before they can use them, and most that I've seen are high in K and low in actual value.

gif animation

So GIF animations (otherwise known as animated GIFs or multi-part GIFs) don't really add functionality to a web site, but they are an easy-to-create, easy-to-download attribution. If made properly, like a GIF should be, they can be of amazingly small size. For updated information from the king of GIF animations, hang a click over to Royal Frasier's GIF Animation on the WWW site (http://member.aol.com/royalef/gifanim.htm).

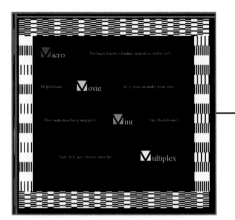

The MicroMovie MiniMultiplex (`http://www.teleport.com/~cooler/MMMM/MMMM.html`) is a virtual entertainment center that won't let your eyes down. Besides using GIF animations in a nifty way of its own (by resizing the GIFs using HEIGHT and WIDTH tags to greatly warp the size of the GIFs pixels), MMMM houses links to many other cool sites using animated GIFs.

Don Barnett's Urban Evening Insect Theatre at `http://www.cris.com/~nekton/barnett.html`, is a clever and entertaining example of an inobtrusive, yet entertaining GIF animation. The bugs are the only part of the whole page's image that move. The lamp is part of a bigger-than-screen-size background tile.

the amazing factor: Hey, if I can do them, anyone can. GIF animations, if created with low K images, don't take up much room overall, and shorten download time for viewers.

the annoyance factor: Because almost anyone can do them, you'll find them everywhere. The "bad" aspect is that most people create GIF animations that loop—meaning they play over and over and over again. Which means that down in your status bar, at least in current browsers, you'll see a

183

constant readout of "42%... 56%... 69%... etc... of 23K" over and over and over again, which can disrupt navigational cues and make it harder to get to where you want to go. The downloading and replaying of a looping GIF animation will probably also curtail the downloading of other page parts, making overall page–loading time add up.

client pull

Client pull is a way of taking over your viewers' browsers and taking them to the URLs you want them to see. Using the <META> tag, basically, your code is telling your viewer's browser to refresh after a certain time, or takes it to the next page in your site, or back and forth among pages— depending on what you've coded it to do.

the amazing factor: Client pull is relatively easy to set up, and you can control how people enter or see all or parts of your site.

the annoyance factor: Viewers could easily get annoyed if they are forced to watch as their browsers are taken over for them, dragging them potentially deeper and deeper into a site with no apparent escape. Use client pull with care.

server push

Server push just isn't as popular as it used to be. Why? Because animated GIFs came along, and suddenly you don't need to know how to program in C++ in order to get an animation on your web page. It's difficult to even find good examples of server push anymore, since many designers have converted over to using animated GIFs to create their wares.

Witness some of the many server-push performances at ParkBench (http://found.cs. nyu.edu/parkbench/performance.html).

the amazing factor: Server push is useful for creating an animation on screen without having to force the viewers page to continually redraw. It's also supported by good ol' browsers like Netscape 1.1.

the annoyance factor: If you know how to program in C++, then perhaps it's not annoying at all. Sure, you can download apps to help you make them, but it's still easier to create GIF animations.

vrml

Virtual Reality Modeling Language, otherwise known as V–R–M–L or "vermull," isn't new news—it just isn't all that practical yet. We'd all think it would be great, say, if we went to a real estate site to check out houses in a city to which we're being relocated, and we could walk from room to room, look out the windows, see what kind of shingles were on the roof, and so on. Or we could visit countries we've always wanted to go to, and wander through villages and into shops to see (and perhaps purchase) merchandise. We'd never have to leave the house again.

the amazing factor: Designers can create "walk throughs" of anything from an office space to an entire city or planet or whathaveyou.

185

the annoyance factor: VRML simply isn't practical yet, at least over the web, because either the images aren't that detailed (in order to save download time), or it's used for reasons that aren't that apparent: it seems that sites using VRML are merely trying to experiment and show that they can do it. Not to mention that if we did use it for a use, such as the real estate example, it would probably take too long to create the site—the house would be sold long before you could create a VRML representation that was detailed enough to inspire someone to send in a bid.

summary

The key to using special effects is to use them wisely. If they contribute to your message, then they make sense. If they have potential to annoy your viewers with extra wait time, or looping beyond their control, then you've got a problem. Technology—and pushing technology to its limit—is cool. But ask yourself if that's really what your visitors need, want, or expect from your site.

advertisements & sponsorship

designing around the hand that feeds

"Advertising may be described as the science of arresting human intelligence long enough to get money from it."

— Stephen Butler Leacock

The other day, I saw an ad for Infoseek, one of the prominent internet search engines (http://www.infoseek.com/) on the side of a San Francisco city bus. Suddenly I had a flashback to the pre-launch of *Wired* magazine, when I lived in New York City—seeing its ads on the sides of buses everywhere I went. First it's hipno-techno-magazines advertising on the sides of buses, then a few years later, it's web sites advertising on the sides of buses. You can't get away from it.

If you're a profit-oriented web site, such as a magazine, informational resource, or whathaveyou, chances are you've realized that the only way a site can really pay for itself is to sell ad space on your site. Whether you decide to call it "ad space" or a "sponsor showcase," whatever it ends up being, it takes up space.

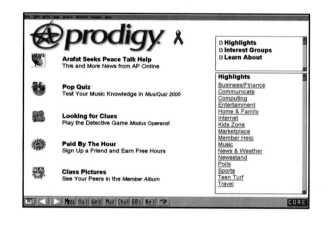

Ever been on Prodigy? Prodigy, even with its recent so-called improvements, still has a funky-looking, slower-than-other-services graphical interface. Despite its clunky history, it has the honor of being the first major online service to have worked ads into its interface. Even back in the black and white monitor days, nearly every section you went to had an advertisement for something for which you had to wait for in order to see the actual menu or content of an area. This, while perhaps a good thing for the advertisers, soon became a thorn in Prodigy members' sides, and a major complaint against Prodigy that I've heard ever since I've been a member (the only reason I kept an account is because I've written about online services for years). If a service is slow to begin with, and I'm paying for the service by the hour, why should I have to wait for an ad to draw on my screen? Despite this sour taste that preempted the scourge of online advertising, it has now become a pretty matter-of-fact that advertising on the web is a viable way to entice potential customers. And we can learn from Prodigy's experience.

According to an article in *Internet Week* (October 31, 1995), "The typical Internet user spends five hours and 28 minutes a week surfing, retrieving files, and otherwise delving into the worldwide network of computer net–works. The time spent by the roughly 10 million regular users of the Net works out to 35 minutes per person over the age of 16 in the U.S. and Canada… Daily, about 7 million people make some use of the Net, Nielsen [the marketing survey company that we usually associate with television] says. The users are affluent, educated and professional. About 25 percent have incomes more than $80,000, compared with 10 percent of the popula-tion as a whole, for instance. Roughly 2.5 million users of the Web have pur-chased a product or service." With numbers like these, it's no wonder that advertising on the web is a big deal nowadays. If you've spent any amount of time on the web, you've run into them. After a while, they become com-monplace, something easy to ignore—which, if you have ever worked for an ad agency or have sold ads for a magazine or site, is not a good thing.

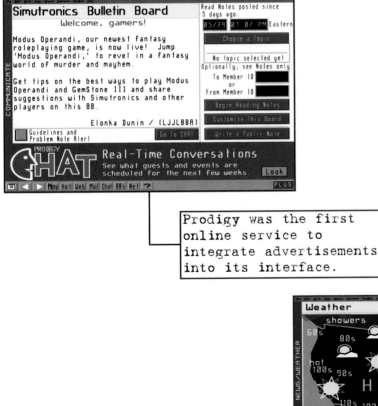

Prodigy was the first online service to integrate advertisements into its interface.

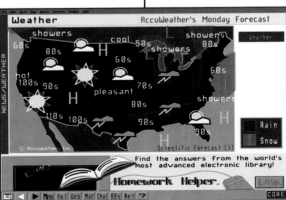

189

Zima was among the first to advertise extensively on the web.

The first advertisement I ever saw on the web (and so did many others) was one for that strange, alcoholic, yuppie-targeted beverage we all affectionately know as Zima, that appeared on the then-unique HotWired site. At the time, I was teaching a web page-making class at San Francisco State University, and one of our class exercises was to critique the ad. Did it annoy us? Yes. Did it confuse us? Yes. Did we get anything out of it? Well, no. Back in the old days (two years ago), this ad confused people new to the web—clicking on it brought viewers to something totally non-HotWired, and yet it was difficult to tell whether or not the ad section was an ad or a part of the online magazine. Many of us are used to seeing ads and can recognize them when we see them, but I'd prefer to have ads and advertising sections clarified so that the bridge between editorial and advertising is clearly marked.

where the ads go

Look through a popular consumer magazine such as *Cosmopolitan* or *Time* or *People*, and you'll notice that big companies and big ads have prime placement: inside the front cover, near the front of the magazine, on the back cover, within important cover-story features. These places are prime real estate for ad sales because they are the most-looked at areas in magazines.

On web sites, it would be easy to understand why prime ad placement tends to be at the very top of the front page or at the very top of subsequent departments. It's the first thing that appears onscreen when someone hits the page. Why buy an ad on a site if it's placed way down below content, where someone has to scroll down to see it... especially if there's a risk that they may click on something and leave the page before they even get all the way down there?

In a very informal survey, it looks like most of the ads on web pages show up at the very top of the page. Some show up at the bottom, but in those cases (ideally, in any case, for the advertiser) the web page is short—with no scroll bar—so that the ads show up on the main screen without any troublesome scrolling that ad buyers may be worried about. Sometimes, but rarely, ads fall in the middle of the text of a page. In any case, most sites give up the valuable first–sight on–site to the powers that pay the price.

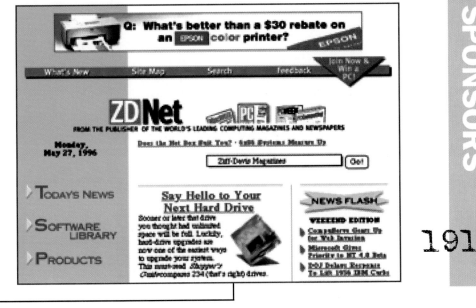

Both c|net and ZDNet place advertisements on the top of their sites' pages, and in both cases, the ads are usually the first image to draw.

People magazine places its advertisements on the bottom of its pages, but since they fall within a standard browser screen (of a 14-inch monitor), the viewer doesn't have to scroll down to view the advertisement.

Playboy's first page hosts three advertisements with bottom-of-the-page placement; only one of which is viewable without scrolling on a standard screen.

what price, ads?

Ad placement in a place where people will actually see it is important. Even as an editor who has been annoyed when ads fall in the middle of stories, or who has had to cut a page because a salesperson sold the space, I've understood that my rent has been paid by advertisers for many years. But you don't need to sell out in order to sell ads. You just need to make your ads a smooth part of the page, hope that it doesn't interfere with a viewer's experience and interaction with your page, and also hope that the content of the ad is relevant to your audience in order to make ad placement work.

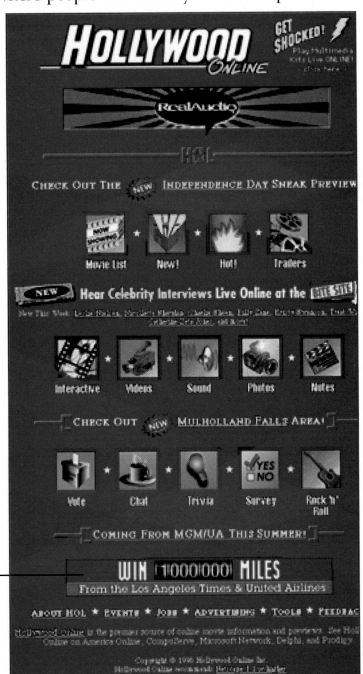

Hollywood Online's advertisement is way, way, way down at the bottom. Advertisers may not be too pleased if viewers are forced to scroll three screens worth in order to view its ad.

193

The most annoying ads utilize the same annoying effects that hamper good design in a web page. They might include an animation that loops so quickly your viewer doesn't have the window–of–time opportunity to click on a link to where they want to go. It might be so large in file size that it significantly slows down the load time of your page and people won't want to return.

the ad design specs (well, sorta...)

The ads that seem most successful in their non–interference with editorial (meaning any content on the page that is not an advertisement) seem to fall in the size range of 6.5 inches wide by about .75 inches in height; some slightly smaller, some slightly bigger, and maintain a file size of about six to 10 kilobytes, which guarantees a fast load time. This size range, most notably the width, falls within the default window size of most popular browsers, such as Netscape Navigator and Microsoft Internet Explorer. The following banner advertisements are labeled with their K sizes and dimensions:

15k - 7.639 by .694 inches (550 by 50 pixels)

9k - 6.667 by .833 inches (480 by 60 pixels)

9k - 6.667 by .833 inches (480 by 60 pixels)

9k - 6.5 by .833 inches (468 by 60 pixels)

6k - 6.611 by .75 inches (476 by 54 pixels)

a unique advertising design example

A unique twist on the web advertising model appears on the Lumiére site (http://www.lumiere.com/), an online magazine about fashion and other popular trendy hip stuff targeted toward the X-gen market. Once the splash screen of the main part of the site finishes its transformation into an entry point (it has an animation that goes from a basic "Lumiére" logo to one that sports an image, headlines, and teasers into the articles inside), the viewer clicks straight into a full page animated advertisement—much like turning the page in a paper magazine. I have yet to figure out why this isn't annoying as hell; maybe it's because of its uniqueness that I sit through its multi-frame show. **The benefit:** no matter what, people will see the ad. Even at low modem speeds, the animation is quick and to the point. As much as it might hamper my linkage to the main part of the site, it's not annoying enough to make me want to write to the site manager and rag on them. It doesn't loop, it doesn't appear in the middle of text I want to read, advertising "interruptions" don't fall between each page I want to access, and it's simply very well designed.

This banner appears before anything else on the page, and gives us the immediate option to continue into the site rather than watch the advertisement if we choose not to.

Adding the word "advertisement" to this section is a nice touch by the designer. Much like some advertisements in magazines that may easily be confused with editorial content, a simple addition of the word "advertisement" clarifies the line between the two.

Limiting the advertisement's animation to five frames doesn't limit its effectiveness or design. Small file size and ensuring the advertisement doesn't repeat itself endlessly avoids annoying viewers and overloading browsers.

197

other ad positions

An alternative way of handling sponsorship is to dedicate a page solely to it. An icon on the main page of your site that leads viewers to "the companies that sponsor this site" is kind to those who don't wish to spend online bucks waiting for ads to appear, but gives the curious the links to advertisers (AKA sponsors) they desire if they choose to click.

If you think that your site's visitors may not be able to tell if an advertisement is an ad and not part of your site, try an old magazine trick: add the word "advertisement" to the image (like Lumiére's advertisement), or if you provide pages to your advertisers, clarify it's an advertisement by putting the word "advertisement" at the top and bottom of the page.

Some sites put ads on their splash screen (the initial screen you fall upon when you enter its URL), with the explanation that "this week, this site is sponsored by...." (or other applicable text) preceding the advertiser's image. The result: viewers only see it once, and yet advertisers get prime placement.

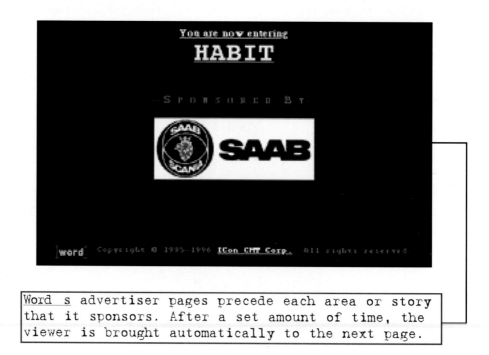

Word's advertiser pages precede each area or story that it sponsors. After a set amount of time, the viewer is brought automatically to the next page.

A variation of dedicating a page solely to a particular advertiser is used on the online magazine *Word's* site (http://www.word.com/). After you click on an article title from the initial screen, a "this section sponsored by" screen appears for enough time (five seconds) for the viewer to see just who it is that paid for the position. The cgi script (<META HTTP-EQUIV="Refresh" CONTENT="5; URL=name of story URL">) on the sponsored–by page then sends viewers into the article that they chose to link to. This method does its job and is effectually inobtrusive.

The Wall Street Journal puts all of its sponsors on one page —out of the way of its main news areas, but always accessible from any page for those who are curious.

199

TIP: ADVERTISING SOFTWARE & SERVICES

There are a bunch of companies, such as NetGravity (http://www.netgravity.com/) and DoubleClick (http://www.doubleclick.net/) appearing on the web-ad horizon that promise to help take care of ad placement based on a site's target audience.

NetGravity's AdServer software is a combination database and scheduling applications that assist a site in placing, rotating, and tracking advertisement hits and results; helpful if different areas of your site are targeted toward various audiences, i.e., a site about baseball, which is targeted toward fans (who may be interested in beer and hotdog advertisements) and players (who may be interested in health food or sportswear). DoubleClick works like an ad agency: you buy space, and depending on your target market, the company determines which ad fits best on that site or page within a site. Rates are dependent on the number of "impressions," or how many times your ad shows up in a given time.

For an updated list of companies who specialize in web advertising software and services, go to http://www.yahoo. com/Business_and_Economy/Companies/Computers/Software/Inter net/World_Wide_Web/Advertising_Management/.

summary

Whether your site is accepting advertising or you're tagged with the task of designing an ad that will be placed on other web sites, the viewer's convenience and bandwidth must be kept in mind. Animation or other effects may seem cool, but they can interfere with a viewer's interaction with a site. Chances are, a viewer comes to your site to find out something specific. If the page is about how to choose the right paint for a kitchen wall, then an ad about Montessori School training is not appropriate. Advertising money may be crucial to keeping your site up and running. But if it interferes with the navigation and usability of your site, it may backfire.

informational exchange tools
the importance of communicating with your public

"The public is a ferocious beast:
One must either chain it up or
flee from it."

– Voltaire

201

There is something unnerving about going to a web site and finding that there are no names of the people who created it, or no way of contacting the authors or owners of a site. I feel like I've just picked up a book and I can't find the author's name anywhere because someone ripped out all of those pages where it was printed.

On the other hand, it can be worse to have sent e-mail to someone or a company to only be ignored. In this instantaneous day and age, if someone doesn't write back to me within 24 hours, it feels like I'm being majorly snubbed.

I'm also a sucker for receiving communication about my site or sites I've worked on, whether they are critiques or kudos about the artwork, layout, navigability, broken links, or whatever. It's not always true that the customer is always right (like the person who wrote to me to suggest that I post pictures of myself in my high school cheerleading costume), but your site's viewers (AKA customers) should always have a way to give their two cents. After all, your site did just take up some of their spare and/or valuable time, or is about to.

what do you need to know?

Before you decide what format your communication tools will take, it helps to know what it is you want from your viewers. For example, I don't really have any need to know my viewers' marital status, or credit card numbers, or snail-mailing address and phone number. All I've needed on my site is mailto: links that I've customized so that when, for example, you're in the gallery, and you want to send me a suggestion for a gallery addition or make a comment, the e-mail is addressed to gallery@typo.com. I have my e-mail program set up to filter the e-mail that comes in from the specific areas of my site, so those sent from the gallery mailto: link go into a mailbox called "gallery." Those from the talent-for-rent section (talent@typo.com) go into a mailbox called "talent."

If you're willing to simply use mailto: as your basis for communication with your audience, then give as much instruction as is necessary for each e-mail link given. For example, if you list chris@company.com and bob@company.com all by themselves with no explanation, who do people write to if they're interested in signing up for a newsletter? Who do they write to if they find out a link is broken, and they want to let the site's owner know about it? Customizing e-mail addresses, such as "info@company.com", "sales@company.com" or "webmaster@company.com" helps, but it doesn't hurt to include explanations such as "For product information and a brochure, send your snail-mail address to sales@company.com" or "To report broken links or technical difficulties with this site, write to webmaster@company.com." A few words make a big difference.

forms & function

Forms offer a flexible way to receive specific information about specific topics, and can be wonderfully simple or amazingly complex. The worst ones are those that ask a person to fill out a bazillion spaces of information before they can even find out what they're filling out the form to do. The best give plenty of explanation about why a user should fill out the form, what they'll get out of it, and guide the viewer through each step with explanations. Figure out what info you want—or need from your audience. A few reasons you'll want to use forms includethe following:

● to get orders

● to receive customer responses

● to ask survey questions

● to find out who came to your site

● to fulfill requests for your business or product information (in the case of forms, this could also mean creating a front-end for a search engine)

● to force password access

● to create an e-mailing list

● to create a snail-mailing list

● to create online tests or contests

● to ask for feedback on the site

seductions & incentives

If you've decided to require registration at your site or have decided to assign passwords to visitors, will people feel it's worthwhile filling out forms or giving you personal information to get at your site's content? I get extremely annoyed at "empty" password–protected sites, or sites that make me register (home address, sex, salary, marital status, employment info, phone numbers, the works) only to lead me to a site that is full of "under construction" signs or outdated information. If you're going to make people work to get into your site, give them a good payoff.

Another pet peeve: if I'm forced to register, but I have no idea what kind of benefits I'll receive by becoming a site's "member." Give potential members a bit of information up front. Even if they've never been to your site before, someone else's badly designed site may have turned them off to registering. Even if you're asking for information simply for your internal marketing statistical purposes, or if you plan on sending everyone who registers your latest product catalog, *let people know*. Honesty is better than just asking people to fill out forms for no apparent reason.

You know how it is when you want information from a simple link and it's not there; it's even more annoying to have filled out a page of questions only to enter an area that has nothing of obvious value. For example, I went to a site that lists itself in Yahoo as a site for a high–falootin web design conference. It took at least 20 minutes to fill out the form, which asked questions about my marital status and yearly income and home phone number (what in the world do they need that information for?), then I was assigned an ID (rather than getting to choose my own) that is impossible for a mere human to remember (it's something like *84f592stbm6*). Whew! I was finally allowed into the site, only to be met with outdated information —the conference was six months ago, and there was no new information about the upcoming conference except a date, which was already posted in the non–passworded area. The mailto: address didn't work (of course, by this time, I didn't want information, I just wanted to complain). And they expect me to pay over $1,000 to go to their web design conference? Yeah, right.

c|net's member registration form is straightforward and quick to fill out, even as long as it is. They've also included reassurances that information will be kept private, and tell us what they'll be doing with the information they're gathering. However, it would be nice to see this information closer to the top of the site, along with more explanation about just what unique privileges we'll get as members. Note how some of the information has default choices checked (such as when you're asked if you want to receive the c|net newsletter), but others, such as what modem you use, are left unchecked. c|net's done a good job of asking applicable marketing questions while leaving irrelevant questions out.

Have you given your viewers the option to keep their information private? If I'm required to fill in my phone number, I don't want to worry about sales people calling me, or other companies "buying" my information for their use.

c|net's registration process includes a privacy notice that explains how it will never give out a member's information unless the member requests that it do so. It also includes an explanation for all its questions, as well as informing its viewers exactly what the company is planning to do with the information it gathers: use the information to compile demographic information in order to sell advertisements. Here's their quote:

205

"c|net online will make no attempt to associate any of the information provided... with anything other than a c|net online username, even if you have entered your first and last name... No information about any member will ever be shared with a third party unless you specifically request it. We collect this information... [to] allow us to customize the service for each individual member's preferences; [and] it helps c|net online and our advertisers understand the demographic profile of our membership. This is essential to keeping the service free to our members." That's easy enough information to provide.

staying in formation

Forms can be functional or frustrating, but most of the ick–factor I've seen comes from those forms that lack consistent design, unfamiliar cues, or bad layout.

Elements available in web forms now include text fields, lists, check buttons, pop–up menus, radio buttons, and other stuff that can be edited, chosen, or filled in by your visitors. The information you need helps to determine the type of form tag you'll use.

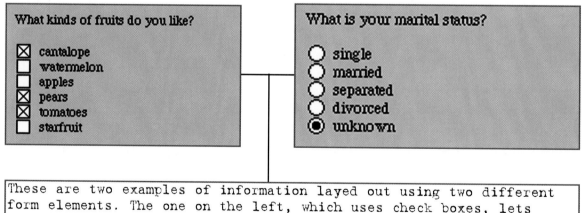

These are two examples of information layed out using two different form elements. The one on the left, which uses check boxes, lets viewers make as many choices as they like out of those provided. The one on the right, which uses radio buttons, allows the viewer to pick only one out of all the choices.

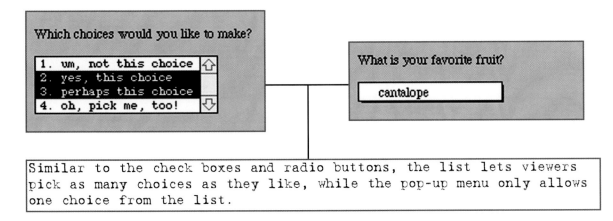

Which choices would you like to make?

```
1. um, not this choice
2. yes, this choice
3. perhaps this choice
4. oh, pick me, too!
```

What is your favorite fruit?

```
cantalope
```

```
Similar to the check boxes and radio buttons, the list lets viewers
pick as many choices as they like, while the pop-up menu only allows
one choice from the list.
```

Which one would you use if you want someone to pick out all the people in a list they had heard of? Of course, you'd want to give them more than one choice. If you need to find out their salary range, marital status, or any topic within a specific range in which they can have only one answer, then radio buttons or pop–up menus are the obvious choice.

consistency and logic

Think of how you have almost always filled out forms. There are certain things that we expect to come in certain order. Let's say all I want to know from you is your name, mailing address, and phone number. Wouldn't you be annoyed if I created a form that asked for your information in this order?

state:
last name:
home phone number:
apartment number:
zip code:
street address:
work phone number:
first name:
city:

It would also be annoying, for example, if I made the "city" field a list of every town and city in the country instead of allowing you to type it in (you'd have to scroll through thousands of choices before you found yours). Lots of sites do this with just the 50 states, and it's a painful process. I'd rather type in the two letters myself than have to reach over to my mouse, click on the pop–up, scroll to my state (so, yeah, now it's only in the "C"s, but what if I still lived in Vermont?). Simplicity is better than multiplicity.

Contact person's name:
`Crystal Waters`
Address Line 1:
`1234 Any Street`
Address Line 2:
`Apt. 1`
City:
`San Francisco`
State:
`CA`
ZIP Code:
`94444`
Phone number:
`415 555 5555`
Contact person's email address:
`crystal@typo.com`

SIRIUS CONNECTIONS

Account Registration

If you would like to order an account with Sirius Connections, please provide the following information:

First, Last Name
Company (optional)
Street Address
City
Zip
Day Phone
Evening Phone
Best time to call
◉ daytime ○ evening
Fax
Existing email

Your Username:
Usernames should be eight characters or less.
Your username is used to log into Sirius and as your email address for sending email.
yourname@sirius.com

Preferred User Name #1
Preferred User Name #2
Preferred User Name #3

Account type :
PPP 14.4K dialup account
PPP 28.8K dialup account

Choice of payment:
◉ Pay each month :$15.00 for 14.4K / $20.00 for 28.8K
○ Pay 6 Months in advance: $75.00 for 14.4K / $100.00 for 28.8K

There is a one-time $35.00 setup fee for setting up PPP account

Your Computer System
Mac
Windows 3.x
Windows 95
Unix
Other

[Send] [Start Over]

```
These form examples show log-
ical order and organization
of form information and usage
of one-choice vs. multiple
choice elements. Note how the
second form not only uses
logical order, it uses group-
ing of common questions, and
easy to read alignment for
better navigation.
```

summary

Communication goes both ways. This doesn't mean that you have to write back to everyone who writes to you or send a thank–you note to everyone who signs your guest book, but you should read what people have to say. Once in a while a gem of a suggestion comes along that, when implemented, greatly enhances your site.

No matter what way you choose to incorporate a feedback or informational mechanism, logical organization and structure will only increase its value to both you and your visitors. Only ask what you really need to know, and explain why you need to know it. The customers may not always be right, but they do need a place to mouth off.

viewing choices

beauty is in the eye of the browser

"If God dwells inside us, like
some people say, I sure hope He
likes enchiladas, because that's
what He's getting!"

— Jack Handy

211

The other day I received an e-mail from a writer with whom I used to work when I was still an editor in New York years ago. I had stumbled across his web page while doing some research, so I dropped him a note to say hello. He wrote back the next day, telling me how he'd followed some of my work in the various magazines I'd written for since we last spoke, and that he'd visited my web page. "By the way," he advised, "you may want to visit your own site with an ASCII-only browser... a lot of the links aren't accessible that way."

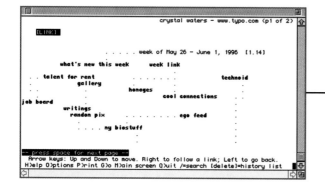

Here's my site's menu page, http://www.typo.com/, as viewed through a Telnet connection. Not all pages in my site function as well as this one in a text-only browser.

An ASCII-only browser? Do these things still exist? Well, yes they do, believe it or not. As web designers, should we care about them at all since they represent such a small portion of the web-viewing public? If the web-viewing audience can't download Netscape, to hell with them, right?

While this isn't really my opinion, a lot of designers would agree with that last statement. Depending on your audience, it may very well be a waste of time—or at least not worth the person-power—to recreate a site in a text-only format. But in some cases, it is worth the trouble to at least download a text-only browser to see what your site looks like in its grasp.

BrowserWatch

BrowserWatch, http://browserwatch.iworld.com/, keeps a constant update on browsers and developers, plug-ins, browser statistics, and more.

download this, do that

Suggesting that users download a
bunch of stuff in order to view
your site may seem like a nice suggestion, but it's a drag to have to
see these icons all over the web.

Some sites handle the problem of designing for multiple browsers by throwing in a caveat that their site is viewable by Netscape or Internet Explorer only, and add links to Netscape and Microsoft for viewers "convenience."

Other sites ask us to widen our windows, change our typefaces, or stay away if we only use the AOL browser. There are some sites that are worth doing this for; others simply strike me as being selfish.

beware of over-designing

I recently consulted for a commercial educational software site whose audience consists mainly of college–level academic and administration personnel. They wanted to redesign their site with Java jazz, Shockwave files, image maps, frames, forms, and every other trick in the book. Fine, I said, but first look at who's coming to dinner.

Most of the people I know who attend or work at universities still access the Internet through a text–based shell account or Unix terminal. In this case, going to the trouble of presenting product information, sales contacts, and customer service info in a text–based format was highly recommended, because an undetermined number of their present and potential customers won't be able to access its wealth of goodies otherwise.

Even something as simple as adding a graphic without any other navigational cues can throw a wrench into the stew if your intended viewers can't see it.

The client doesn't need to forego any sort of fancy stuff if they want to impress those potential customers who do view their site with a browser that supports all the gizmos. Balance, in this case, is the key.

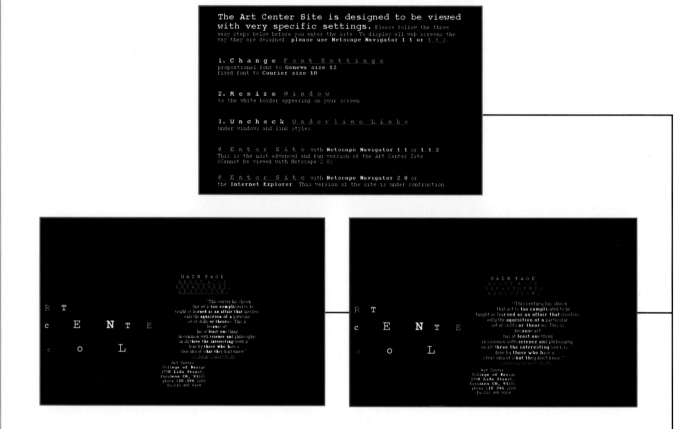

The Art Center College of Design site (http://www.artcenter.edu/) demands a lot from its visitors. First of all, you have to change your proportional font to Geneva (a Mac-only typeface) size 12, and your fixed font to Courier size 10. Then you're asked to resize your window; then uncheck "underlined links." There are two different versions of the site; one for Netscape 1.1 and 1.1.2, and another for Netscape 2.0 and Internet Explorer.

If you don't follow its directions, Art Center's main page looks like the image on the bottom left. By following the directions, you see the image on the right.

how far do you go?

You've probably noticed that some sites that offer forms for its viewers to fill out also offer the option to send e-mail if the viewer's browser doesn't support forms. It's also true that some browsers still don't support the mail-to: tag, which enables the viewer to click on an e-mail address and an e-mail window pops up. Adding the option of sending e-mail from another application may be the only extra convenience you need to offer.

Then there are those of us who find frames annoying and wish more sites presenting information in frames would also offer a no-frame viewing choice, even if we use a browser that supports frames.

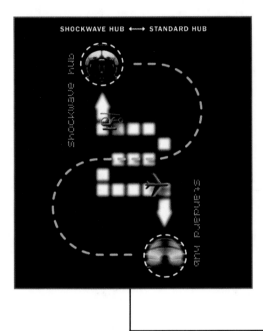

```
Qaswa Air (http://www.qaswa.com/)
offers a choice between a
Shockwaved and a standard version
of its site.
```

```
the place, by Joseph Squier
(http://gertrude.art.uiuc.edu/
ludgate/the/place.html),
includes this caveat:
"Because of its heavy reliance
on graphics, text-only brows-
ing is not recommended at the
place. The place was developed
on a Mac, and is optimized for
viewing on that platform. The
preferred mode of transporta-
tion is Netscape."
```

215

This is the trouble with an interface that has no standards. It's true that the Netscape–enhanced "standard" certainly is the most popular, but there are still a number of other browsers out there, and some of them read the same tags the same way, some completely misinterpret the tags, and some don't read them at all. I set up a page on my "free" America Online web page space that looks pretty simple and straightforward when viewed through Netscape Navigator, but when viewed on AOL's now–infamous browser, it looked simply and straightforwardly like crap. While I'm generally a Navigator snob, it did bother me that those poor AOLers were faced with a site that talked about web site design, but that looked attrocious.

```
c r y s t a l   w a t e r s

AKA CrystalW@aol.com

just click back or next to go through this site page by page, or
go directly to:
. . . . . . . . . . . . . my    et al
. . . . . . . . . . . .        links
. . . . . . . . . . . . . bizarre-o-rama
. . . . . . . . . . . . . tattoo you; tattoo me
. . . . . . . . . . . . . digital stories
. . . . . . . . . . . . . litrachure (sure...)
. . . . . . . . . . . . . cool cool sites

To find out more about me, drop into my staff page at The Net.

<-- b a c k . . . . . . . . . . . . . . . . . . . . . . . n e x t -->
```

A site designed for Netscape can look significantly different—or just different enough—to look nothing like you intended it to. Here's a test site I did designed for Netscape above a shot of how it looks when viewed with the AOL for Mac Browser v1.1.

```
crystal   waters
_____

AKA CrystalW@aol.com
_____

just click back or next to go through this site page by page, or go directly to:
.........my bio et al
.........webcentric links
.........bizarre-o-rama
.........tattoo you; tattoo me
.........digital stories
.........litrachure (sure...)
.........cool cool sites
_____

To find out more about me, drop into my staff page at The Net.
_____

................. n e x t -->
```

summary

No matter what browser or browsers you decide to design for, it's a good idea to download a few others to check out how they show your page. It could be that a quick and not–so–big change to your layout could make your site multi-browser happy.

Here are some sites where you'll find alternate browsers for download. Note that some may be trial versions that you'll only be able to use for a limited time unless you purchase the product. But for testing, 30 days or so should be enough.

```
Windows

Cello - http://www.law.cornell.edu/cello/cellotop.html

NCSA Mosaic for Microsoft Windows -
http://www.ncsa.uiuc.edu/SDG/Software/WinMosaic/HomePage.html

winWeb - http://galaxy.einet.net/EINet/WinWeb/WinWebHome.html

QuarterDeck Mosaic - http://arachnid.qdeck.com/

Microsoft Internet Explorer - http://www.microsoft.com

Netscape Navigator - http://home.netscape.com/

WebSurfer - http://www.netmanage.com/netmanage/softgallery.html

SPRYNET Mosaic - http://www.sprynet.com/

Macintosh

NCSA Mosaic for the Apple Macintosh -
http://www.ncsa.uiuc.edu/SDG/Software/MacMosaic

MacWeb - http://galaxy.einet.net/EINet/WinWeb/WinWebHome.html

Microsoft Internet Explorer - http://www.microsoft.com/

Netscape Navigator - http://home.netscape.com/

Apple Cyberdog - http://cyberdog.apple.com/

WebSurfer - http://www.netmanage.com/netmanage/softgallery.html
```

test driving your site

a comprehensive before-going-live checklist

"I never blame failure — there are
too many complicated situations in
life — but I am absolutely merci-
less toward lack of effort."

— F. Scott Fitzgerald

When's the last time you bought a car without taking it for a test drive first? Never, I assume. Just as it's crucial to test out products before you buy them, it's imperative to test out your site before you make a huge announcement to thousands of people (or even 10 people) about how wonderful and great it is, and how it will serve their every need from now on. While you may have no intention of making these claims in the first place, I'm sure you've received announcements of this sort, and gone to the site, only to be met with a bunch of links that go nowhere, or images that won't load, or you get into the middle of the site and can't find your way back.

upload and test

Your site may work great when it's running off your hard drive, but how will it work from your server or your service provider's server? The only way to find out is to try it.

One common problem is due to the designer setting up the site structure differently on the home drive than on the remote server. When you're creating a site that has links to images or pages in other folders or directories, then the anchor tags (the http ones) to those links must match once your pages are on the other system. For example, if your background image is called "tile.gif," and you kept—and referred to—it in a separate folder/directory called "images," then there must also be a folder/directory on your server called images, in the same relative position as on the drive on which you designed the site.

try your site with images off

Some people prefer to cruise the web with image-loading turned off, so that they can get around faster. When they hit a site of interest, they then turn on image loading. So how does your site look when there's no images showing? Do your pages come up as blanks with no navigational tools to be found?

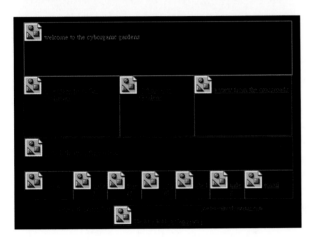

If you haven't put ALT tags in your image codes, now's the time. This tag inserts a line of text if the image doesn't load, so at least people can hopefully get an idea where that link will take them.

If you have inserted ALT tags, do they make any sense? If they are simply the name of the graphic, or one word non-navigation explanations (i.e. "graphic.gif" or "this is an image map"), then they do very little to help out your visitors.

hows it look in other browsers?

I know, I advocate the use of Netscape Navigator or Microsoft Explorer, since they give more flexibility and options in web site design, but what if, by chance, some poor soul comes wandering to your site using another browser?

And if you've gone to the trouble of creating multiple versions of your site, say, one for browsers that support frames, and one that doesn't, check to make sure your alternative site works in its applicable browser. You may be surprised at what you're seeing—or not seeing at all.

As mentioned in the Viewing Choices chapter, there are still a good chunk of people who use text–only browsers. Even if you don't create a text–only design, testing your site with a text–only browser is a great way to test the overall navigability and "understandability" of your site.

how s it look on other platforms?

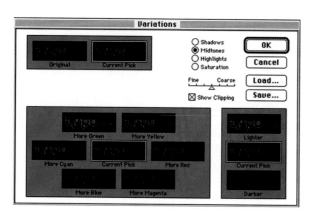

You may think that if you've designed your site on a Macintosh, and tested everything on Netscape Navigator for the Mac, that every–thing will look hunky–dory on the Windows version of Navigator. T'aint always so.

Graphics, for example, often show up darker on a Windows monitor. You may want to go back to your graphics application and alter your images' contrast so that they are more easily viewed on various platforms.

TIP: HTML FOR ALL

A resource for practical information on designing a site for multiple browsers is Hybrid HTML Design: A Multi-Browser HTML Reference by Kevin Ready and Janine Warner (New Riders Publishing). You'll find over 400 pages that show examples of sites in a variety of browsers, in-depth reviews of HTML editors and how they rate in the tags department, and what seems like every HTML tag known dissected for your designing pleasure.

keep text and links readable on the background

This is a very easy thing to check, and it's very logical to figure out what's wrong and what has to be done. If you can't read the text, the people coming to your site won't be able to, either. The most important key to readability is contrast. If your type color is light, make your background dark, and vice versa.

If you use background tiles that have both light and dark colors in it, neither light or dark text will read very easily over it. Make sure your tiles are either overall light or dark—the opposite of whatever color text you're using.

color by numbers

A lot of people prefer to work in their graphics programs or browse the web using the highest monitor setting that their computer supports. But there are still quite a few people whose computer's color limit is 256, especially on older systems. Before you set your site loose on the world (ideally, you did this when developing the graphics in the first place) give it a look–through with your monitor set at 256 colors and the lowest resolution your video card supports.

And don't forget the browser–safe color palette mentioned in the Mood Lighting chapter. If you didn't use this palette, you probably have dithered colors in your images or background tiles.

are images as small as they can be?

Did you save all of your GIFs in GIF89a format? Whether you decided to make a color of your image transparent to make it seem as though it's float-ing above the background or not, saving your image in GIF89a format could cut your image size down to as much as half. There are a number of applications available to translate GIF87a format to GIF89a, and lots of commercial and shareware applications, such as Fractal Painter and LViewPro, allow you to save–as to the GIF89a file format.

—— Don't forget to test your JPEGs at different levels of compression—the higher the quality, the bigger the file.

```
TIP: DESIGNING WEB GRAPHICS

    For a great resource on creating graphics for the
web, pick up a copy of Designing Web Graphics by
Lynda Weinman. Not only does it cover the intrica-
   cies of designing 8-bit graphics and making back-
ground tiles, you'll also find a wealth of tips on how to
make images as small as possible while retaining as high
as quality as possible, image map how-tos, alignment
issues, and oh so much more.
```

cover your tracks

Like any good web designer, you've stolen HTML code from sites that you like (that's what View Code is for, right?). Well, if you make a practice of this, make sure that all links are changed to reflect what's in your site, and not the persons you stole it from. I wrote an article for *The Net* magazine called "Steal My Web Page"—and a lot of people did. How do I know? I did a search for my name in Lycos (http://www.lycos.com/), and up popped a whole list of people who obviously stole the code—because my name was still in the title bar!

Which leads us to...

CHAPTER 15   TESTING

title bar matching

Do the titles in your title bars match the contents of your page? If you've cut and pasted code from other pages (even your own), to save time and because the basic structure of each page is the same, make sure to change the words within the <title> </title> tags.

It's especially important to make your title bars descriptive, because when someone bookmarks your page, the title bar words are what show up as the site description in the bookmark listing. For example, instead of calling your home page "Welcome to Our Company Page" or "My Home Page," consider titling it "Acme Home Page" or "Bob Smith's Web Site" or "Zebra Museum Site Main Index"... anything to differentiate it from the possibly hundreds of other listings in someone's bookmark file.

spelll czech!!!

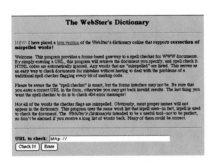

Spell check your pages! If I go to a web site that claims to be a professional organization, and it's full of spelling errors (especially if they misspell their own company or product names—it happens!), I'm less likely to go back to the page, and certainly wonder how professional the organization really is.

If your HTML editor doesn't have a spelling checker, cut and paste the text into your word processor to check for obvious errors, take note of errors, and go back to your editor to fix them.

If you don't have a spelling checker anywhere in your arsenal, after you've loaded your pages to your web server, load up your browser and click over to the WebSter's Dictionary (http://www.eece.ksu.edu/~spectre/WebSter/spell.html). This nifty tool will spell check any URL you enter. It may take some time to go through all of your pages, but isn't it better than losing a customer due to a misspelling?

how fast is fast?

As much as we might not be able to understand why the rest of the world hasn't all purchased 28.8 modems yet, it remains a statistical fact that a high-percentage of modem owners still use their trusty 14.4 to access the web. Another thing to remember, though, is not just potential slow access because people don't want to buy another modem after spending money on a 14.4 a year ago, but that there are still many areas in the U.S. (and I'm sure in other countries, too) where local-access dial-up does not exist. These people are spending at least seven cents a minute on a 14.4 waiting for pages to load. Of course, depending on your goals for your site and your target audience (i.e. you're targeting only people who buy lots of new computer equipment), this may be of little consequence in your site design.

navigation

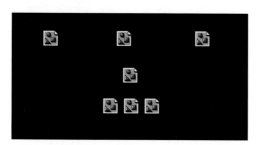

Do viewers have navigational options? Your home page image map may win a cool-web-art award, but is it the only option you give for people to navigate your site? Adding a simple text navigation bar on the page will assist those who don't load graphics, use a text browser, or can't utilize an image map (see page 234 in this chapter to learn about designing sites for the access impaired).

Do you continue to provide navigation tools throughout the site? If someone has wandered into the depths of your content, can they find their way back using the options you've provided? True, every browser I've seen has a "back" button, but don't count on the browser's navigational tools for users to find their way—especially if your site is using frames. Using the browser's "back" button may suck them right out of your site altogether.

ad placement

If you've sold advertisements or sponsorship banners, are they falling in the correct place on the page? And if you've promised an advertiser a particular placement (such as on the top of a specific page related to their service), is it showing up properly? If not, you may end up having a hard time renewing the contract.

alignment

Are images falling in the places that you thought you told them to? Is text wrapping around the images where you want them to wrap? This is especially important to check within other browsers, since many don't support certain common alignment tags.

Within tables and frames, is text in the proper position that makes it the easiest to read? Remember, simple tips like making sure large bodies of text aren't affected by an orphaned <center> tag that got left behind greatly increase readability.

window resizing

Do people have to widen their browser window to get a full look at your site? If you ask them to widen it one time, do they have to widen it again when they hit another page?

Yes, I've been to sites where I need to open my window maybe an inch more than the default size. This isn't so bad, but then I click to go to another page in the site and it's just enough wider that I have to either scroll sideways, or open my window wider again. Sure, opening a browser window a little isn't much work, but a viewer shouldn't have to keep doing it for every page they visit.

is your   cool stuff   gratuitous?

One reason the web, and online services with graphical interfaces (such as America Online), have become so popular is because they can show us pretty pictures rather than just straight text. But before you slather your pages with special effects and big images, make sure they serve a purpose. If the purpose is to show off your artwork or JavaScript finesse, then fine. But if you're putting little JavaScript scrolling messages across the bottom of the screen just because you *can*, you'll end up annoying more people than impressing them: especially after their browser crashes.

do all links work?

It's frustrating to go to a site where you think you're going to be able to find what you want, only to be greeted with an error message because a link doesn't work. Test each and every text link, image map, and image link that you may have.

can they contact you?

Can you imagine handing out a business card that only had your name on it, but no contact information? Make sure all relevant information is included somewhere easily accessible on your site. Mailto: tags are easy to insert, and by now you should be familiar with your company's mailing address, phone numbers, and fax numbers, so that will take 15 seconds to type. If you usually tell customers your street address, put it in. If you'd rather have them call you than e-mail, say that. If there's more than one person that people can write to for a specific purpose, specify the role of each addressee (i.e. "e-mail Sue for sales information, e-mail Anne for technical specifications.").

are links and icons consistent?

Do you use the same link names and icons for an area throughout your site? For example, if you use a compass icon on one page to give people the option to view your site map, do you use the same icon for the same purpose on other pages?

Besides using the same icons, be sure that the ALT tags you've added to an image remain the same for those who aren't viewing or can't view images (again, I'll recommend you read the section, designing sites for the access impaired on page 233, to more fully understand the significance of ALT tags and their consistency). What about placement? If you've decided to put your menu bar on the bottom of pages, make sure it stays at the bottom of pages so people don't have to work to find it.

password protection/registration requirements

HOTWIRED

You are surfing as:

Membername: [   ]
Password: [   ]

☒ Store your membername and password
on the hard drive of the machine
you're using. Note: It's not a
good idea to do this if you share
your computer, since someone other
than you could use your membername
and password.

[log in]

Lots of sites now require viewers to become "members," and require ID and password access to get at the meat of the pages. Asking each person to answer a multitude of survey questions is asking them to do work for you. Not to mention the fact that it's hard enough to remember an ID and password for one online service; now people are expected to remember them for hundreds of web sites.

Have you given a reason up front for asking personal questions? If it's for internal survey reasons, say so. If you're going to sell or share the information to other companies, say so. If it's to track how many times I come to your site, tell me. Honesty is a good thing. And, if only to make me happy, don't ask for personal questions such as salary and home phone numbers if you don't need them for a specific purpose, and haven't told me what it is. And don't forget to give me the option to tell you whether or not I want you to sell or give away my information.

229

are you ready to fulfill your promises?

If you're promising a daily or weekly update to your site, are you prepared to do so? It's better to tell people "we're weekly now, but we'll be going daily in a few months!" than to promise daily updates and not deliver. Just as important is to make sure that if your site is used as a medium to give information about timely subjects, that you upkeep the site in a way that continues to portray your professional image. If you don't have the time or people power to do so, it may be a smarter marketing move to simply take the site down altogether.

another thing about dates

I've only noticed this recently, but there seems to be a number of sites that list events only by month and day, omitting the year in which they are occurring. Sounds silly, perhaps, but now that the web has been widely available for more than a couple of years, it's imperative to include the *year* something is happening. How many times have I seen an event I'm interested in, then click through a few more pages, only to find out it happened in 1993? (not to mention that I then spend too much time commiserating about the reason those pages even exist anymore...)

size warnings

Got a humdinger of a piece of artwork or a long, long text file that your site just can't do without? You don't have to get rid of large files, just warn visitors as much as possible about what's coming up. If it's a 100K image, add whatever "warning" information you can to its link, i.e. "100k JPEG; approx. 2 minutes loading time at 28.8."

There's always the LOWSRC tag that can be used within an image tag to load a lower resolution representation of the higher resolution image.

Long text files also have a pain–in–the–butt quotient. Any file over 20K can be a hassle to wait for, but a 20K text file takes up more room on a page than an image, and so can seem more overbearing.

If you can't break up your text files on to separate pages because your customers may need to print out a full document from their browser (it's inconvenient to have to print info from a number of separate pages), at least give viewers a warning before they click into a deluge of ASCII.

I think it's safe to say that if people know what they're getting into before faced with a large image or hefty web page, and are given the choice to click there or not, they'll be happier. Sometimes, the "stop loading" button just doesn't work.

is your site easy to update?

If your site must be maintained or upgraded on a regular basis, is it easy enough for you to do so without having to wade through random code or start from scratch? Or if you're out sick one day, will someone else be able to open up a coded page and figure out what to do to update it?

Simple additions such as adding spaces (ones your browser won't read) among elements in the HTML code make it easier to see where something gets added or moved. Whether your updating process is automated, or you have to hand–code any changes or additions, put it to the test.

231

can your server handle it?

Now that all your pages are on your server or your service provider's server, give it the test. Try out your pages at peak Internet–access times; usually around lunch hours and after 5:00 p.m. Get as many people you know to access the site at the same time as possible to see if there are any significant lags or "that web site is busy" messages.

If your site is hosted remotely at a service provider, talk to their web administrator about its server performance, and how many people can simultaneously access a page, or if they limit the amount of file transfers per month (my basic site package with my provider, for example, allows one gigabyte of file transfers a month, whether it's lots of little files or a couple of huge ones that people access from typo.com. If I want more, I have to pay more for it.)

under construction signs

The fluidity of the web medium means that probably 99 percent or more of all sites are constantly under construction. People visiting your site won't necessarily be turned off if you happen to have a couple of pages that aren't done yet—but if you do decide to announce the fact that an area or page is under construction, consider the following:

1. Avoid blinking "under construction!" notices. Highlighting your under construction areas brings unneeded attention, and blinking is annoying anyway.

2. If a page is under construction, don't make the link active yet. Someone will probably click your link anyway, even with your notice, and get an error message. A turn off.

3. Put any "under construction" notices up front so that people don't waste their time going to a page just to be welcomed with "thanks for finding this page, but, sorry, we haven't done it yet!"

4. While the icon of the little person shoveling is cute, it's also something a lot of people are sick of, and it may clash with the rest of your design. Besides, no one that I know of can really agree just what it is that the little person is shoveling.

clarity factors

You would think that by now everyone would understand that it's illegal to copy someone else's stuff and put it up on their web page and claim it as their own. Still, it happens. While putting the words "The entire content of this site is © Acme Company 1996 unless otherwise specified" can't prevent a person from cutting and pasting, it may at least make them feel guilty about it.

clarity factors

Is it clear throughout your text what is a new section or paragraph? Don't forget to include subheads where necessary—ones that stand out from the main body of text—and either indent new paragraphs or add <P> paragraph breaks to text. Horizontal rules, while the bane of some web designers, also serve to break up big chunks of text into more readable, discernible sections.

designing sites for the access impaired

While designing for the visually impaired was probably not on your list of goals for your site, not surprisingly, the guidelines for good navigable design also assist in the overall accessibility of your site for those with disabilities. Spending some time reading through those sites whose goal is to help those with disabilities access web-based and other Internet information will open your eyes to some critical information access issues.

Paul Fontaine of the **Center for Information Technology Accommodation** in Washington D.C., has published a document to assist those in designing web pages that are accessible to the visually impaired. *Writing Accessible HTML Documents* (http://www.gsa.gov/coca/WWWcode.htm) is a comprehensive list of guidelines that are easily implemented into a site and do not disturb the overall design or aesthetic quality. Whether your site is specifically targeted toward the visually impaired or you simply wish to make your site accessible, this is a good resource for ideas and sample HTML code.

For example, JPEG images are able to include comments in their files which are readable by some browsers. Include these comments when you can. Some image editors, such as GifConverter for the Mac, allow you to type in JPEG image comments in a pop up dialog window.

Another addition suggested by Fontaine is to include a transcript of any audio files you include on the site. Even if you don't have the person-power to transcribe each

and every audio file, try to at least provide synopses for those who are unable to hear the files on your site.

At the time I'm writing this chapter, Productivity Works' speaking browser, **pwWebSpeak**, was still in beta testing (http://www. prodworks.com/). The browser interprets HTML codes (headers, line breaks, and so on) in a way that allows the user to navigate through the structure of a site based on contents, sentences and paragraphs, and also uses large characters in its display for those partially sighted. Braille output is also an option.

Mike Paciello, founder of **WebABLE** (http://www.webable. com/), not only tackles web accessibility for the visually impaired, but also for those he calls "print impaired"—which include the visually impaired, but also those persons who may be unable to turn printed pages, or use a keyboard or a mouse, because of limited or no use of their hands or fingers. In some cases, people with dyslexia or other cognitive disabilities are included in this category. Paciello's tips include using descriptive ALT tags, text links as well as image links, and advises that designers use the minimum number of links per sentence as possible for easier understanding and navigation.

Interestingly, HTML is the ideal kind of page format coding for text readers. Says Paciello: "...the richness of the description of the document structure is the greatest friend of the blind user, particularly those who use Braille displays or print documents that must be translated to Braille. As a result, HTML is ideal because it provides knowledge about a document's construct that is important to the Braille translation software. Titles, paragraphs, lists, tables, etc....etc... all contain their own formatting constructs. Braille translation software identifies the entity, associates that with a format, and then does the proper translation for the blind user."

The CPB/WGBH

National Center for Accessible Media <u>D</u>

Image Description:
Fading, blue-colored, block letters spell out: "N C A M." Words above and below it read: "The CPB/WGBH National Center for Accessible Media."
<u>Return</u>

The **National Center for Accessible Media** (http://www. boston.com/wgbh/ncam) has ample information on web site captioning (such as captions on QuickTime movie clips), adapting media to the web and other formats, and more.

Note its careful use of ALT tags, as well as the <u>D</u> notations, which take you to detailed image descriptions.

Also of note: **NCSA Mosaic** hosts an Access Page on its site (http://bucky.aa.uic.edu/), which includes information on designing for those with visual, physical, hearing, and cognitive disabilities. The site also includes information for access methods by specific platforms: Windows, DOS, Mac, and X-Windows, and lists newsgroups, sites, and other resources.

Did you know you can design your site to be accessible by phone? One such company promoting a "phone browser" is **NetPhonics** (http://www.netphonics.com/). The Web-On-Call Voice Browser lets people dial in to your web site and search through and receive its information via audio, fax, or e-mail via touch-tone. Intriguing, hmm? Seems logical if you'd like to offer those customers or potential customers who don't use the Internet access to your wealth of company information.

CHAPTER 15

TESTING

235

summary

If there's anything any designer has learned from his or her experience in creating anything, is that there's no way you can get everything right the first time around. As publishers in the web world, we're lucky—if we find a mistake, we can fix it almost instantaneously. Good design shows you care, and taking care of potential problems before you go live will save you numerous headaches later on.

CHAPTER 15

TESTING

web designers' pet peeves

opinions from the trenches

"You never know what is enough
unless you know what is more than
enough."

— William Blake

I should have known, huh? Ask a bunch of designers what their pet peeves are about web design, and you're sure to be deluged with e-mail. The following are some choice peeves from designers of many persuasions, quoted with their permission. "NO BLINK TAGS!"

gratuitous graphic & gizmos

It seems that in the rush to implement all the bells and whistles, designers and, most likely, programmers, are putting in code that is problematic for browsers. As long as that code is there, I'll never see the page and never go back for fear of another computer crash (I don't have collision insurance). I think designers should try to work with the existing browser technology and only try the tricky stuff if they know it works.

```
Jim Sullivan
The Internet Search Assistant
http://www.abbington.com/
```

Graphics that were clearly created to impress a board of directors and that leave ordinary users either staring at a blank screen or moving on to the next site rather than waiting for it to load.

```
Mark Loundy
Southern California Telecommunications Chair, NPPA
http://sunsite.unc.edu/nppa/
```

Something I find annoying in digital design is this tendency to use icons by default rather than text. Somewhere along the line somebody decided that every section of every web site has to have some sort of cute icon, then everyone followed that person. Icons are supposed to represent sections or features of the site visually, in a more direct fashion than text. Most times this is not the case, and the icon art is extremely ugly, or worse, boring and generic.

```
wayne b
with the monks of shaolin
http://www.beatthief.com
```

Peeve: animated GIFs with really quick loop times. They are constantly "reloaded" in Netscape, every half of a second or so, and while they're reloading, they disable all other navigational buttons. So you time it just right, in between reloads, and slam on the stop button, so you can actually move around. It's kind of like hitting the buzzer on a game show.

Jack Lyon
Senior Editor
PC/Computing

Shockwave is merely an attempt to jam a square peg into a round hole.

On an opinionated note—Shockwave is garbage. It feeds into the mentality that fuels sites like PepsiMax and Mission Impossible; namely, that the web is a medium to broadcast CD–ROMs.

It's "extremely powerful" only in that it takes a crucial element of Web design—the interface—and puts it in the hands of multimedia developers, rather than web developers. As a result, we get sites that are, for lack of a better term, mis–designed.

Director is NOT a web development tool. It was never designed to be one. Shockwave is merely an attempt to jam a square peg into a round hole. Its broad acceptance, I think, comes not from its practical usefulness, but rather from being the first multimedia tool out there (pre–Java, GIF89, and streaming video), and already having an established base of Director developers to create content for it. Nevermind that these people aren't necessarily trained in creating content for the web.

When more people realize that you can easily make that logo spin with a GIF89, which is smaller and easier to make, and that mouseover features can be done with itty bitty Java apps, Shockwave will die the slow death it deserves.

Joshua Wolf
World Wide Web Developer, The Princeton Review
http://www.review.com/

CHAPTER 16   PET PEEVES

upgrade your attitude

My web design pet peeve? Web sites that are "enhanced" for anything. It's fine to use a few tags that only render in a specific browser, but not those tags that are unfriendly to the more common web clients. Besides, it looks silly to tell visitors to "Download this new client now!"

```
Rod Montgomery
Web Designer
http://iquest.com/~rod/
```

Here's one of my pet peeves: web pages designed for one browser only with a link telling me to upgrade *NOW!* A little hard since most popular browsers don't run on my platform....

PS: My primary browsing platform is a NeXTStation.

```
Betsy Dunphy
Aesir Computing, Inc.
http://www.aesir.com/
```

groans about graphics

Don't use extremely large image files as your background! It makes loading the page far too tedious. Remember, the beauty of the web is its speed and dynamic nature. Don't ruin it by wasting bandwidth with background images that are unnecessary. There are plenty of beautiful images that are of reasonable size.

```
Steven Smith
consultant/designer
smiths@cis.ohio-state.edu
```

background blues

My pet peeve: background graphics that make it harder to read the fore-ground text. You may have a great design, but if it makes it hard to read your message, it's hurting your image.

```
Ewan Grantham
consultant
http://www.cris.com/~egranthm
```

feedback frustrations

If you're not going to include a customized feedback form on your pages, include a mailto: link at the bottom of every page. It doesn't have to take much room—it can be as simple as "Please send comments to me@here.site.com." I like interacting with the web sites I visit, and this includes sending feedback about the good stuff and the bad that I see. Ignore this, and you're missing out on one of your most valuable sources of input—your audience.

> Don't miss out on one of your most valuable sources of input - your audience.

```
Lisa Reeve
web designer
http://www.quatermass.koan.net/reptile/
```

Many organizations (businesses, educational institutions, nonprofit organizations, web design companies—you name it!) do not put their address, telephone number, and so on anywhere on their site. This practice is extremely frustrating and unhelpful. Off-Internet contact information should appear somewhere on web sites.

```
Erika Miles
Center for Health Care Strategies
http://www.chcs.org
```

241

Be sure to have a convenient mail–to/feedback address that's repeated on every page. Few things annoy me more than having to jump from page to page on a site, just to find out how to report a download problem, 404 error on a link, etc. I've been to sites that have *no* provision for e–mail feedback, and I think that's inexcusable.

```
Celeste Dolan Mookherjee
editor/graphic design
The Underground Informer
http://www.primenet.com/~lonnie/ui/
```

navigation narrow-mindedness

Your users should always know at any given moment where they've been on the site.

The single biggest complaint I have about probably the majority of web sites—and this includes a lot of "big name" outfits—is poorly conceived structure and navigation. Duplicated internal links, missing "home" links, pages that jump all over without any apparent logical consistency—it's a mess much of the time. But so long as they have spiffy graphics, frames, maybe a little Java, we go, "Whoa, kewl site."

I don't care how complex your site is: if it's carefully and thoughtfully designed, your users should always know at any given moment where they've been on the site, and where they have yet to go. It should almost never be necessary to hit your browser's Back button to move around within a site.

```
Brent Eades
http://www.worldlink.ca/almonte/brent
```

readability rules

The web is a challenging reading medium. Chop copy into short paragraphs and help the reader with subheads, pull quotes and appropriately emphasized text. Also, narrow your column widths: <BLOCKQUOTE> is a reader's friend.

```
Pete Johnson
PeteJ@tlg.net
```

Black text on white may seem boring after a while, but if the information isn't holding my attention, changing colors won't do it either. When I take time to read a newsletter (or any document), I'm after the information and I prefer it in dark letters on a light or neutral background in narrow columns. Reversing type on a dark background barely does it for me in ad copy. For a lot of text, forget it. For visual interest, consider adding an occasional graphic in the margin.

```
Chris Hammon
Writer-Producer, Quanta Dynamics, Inc.
http://www.quantadynamics.com/
```

who do you think you are?

There's a very common sin of failing to explain exactly what material a site contains. I don't know how many times a day I connect to sites whose main page consists solely of something like this:

Acme Consulting Services.

Enhanced for Netscape 2.0

Links | Customer Information | Internet | Services | Contacts

Ya know? I mean, what does any of that mean? What are they selling, where do those vague and unhelpful link descriptions lead? Who knows?

243

It would be much better if the designer added a sentence or two to every link description, and a paragraph right up front explaining who you are and what your site is about. But far too few sites seem to bother. The prevailing mentality appears to be, "Well, I know what's in here... I guess my users will figure it out too."

```
Brent Eades
http://www.worldlink.ca/almonte/brent/
```

frames suck

Right up there on my list of web design–don'ts is the gratuitous use of frames. There is nothing more irritating than viewing a site on a small monitor (15 inches or smaller, the way the vast majority of web surfers do) and have a third of the screen be permanently reserved for an unnecessary navigation bar at the bottom of the screen.

```
Margaret Gould Stewart
Creative Director, Tripod Inc.
http://www.tripod.com/
```

```
Frames are just
too annoying.
```

Another pet peeve is (surprise!) frames. They show off the designer's technical expertise, I suppose, but they're ugly and unwieldy. They're just too annoying. I can never figure out how to navigate in them, you can't view the underlying source and figure out how they're done, they're just a pain, and another reason to move on.

```
Willa Cline
http://www.willa.com/
```

get it to the server on time

Yesterday's news makes yesterday's site. Commit to timely publishing and deliver on your commitment. Comb your site regularly for time lapses—coming events which have passed, last year's copyright dates, obsolete URLs, dated software references and no–longer–fresh material. If a page has a "Last updated:" line, keep it current.

Execute good intentions, don't just state them. Sites that say "Keep checking this area for updates," "Coming soon!" and "Under construction" are usually talking to themselves. You won't drive usage on expectations.

Pete Johnson
PeteJ@tlg.net

You won't drive usage
on expectations.

don't conceal content

One of my pet peeves about web design is not putting any content on the home page. Lately I've run across a lot of sites, art sites in particular, with nothing but a cute little button in the middle of the page. Click it, and you get a second page with maybe two cute little buttons, and no indication as to what the links lead to. I generally lose interest at this point.

Willa Cline
http://www.willa.com/

Don't bury your "destination content." That is, if you have an article or a page that is the one most visitors are most likely to want to get to, or if there's one *you* want them to see most, be sure that it's easily accessible from your default or front page. One link away at most. Lots of sites get lured by the excitement of hierarchical hypertext into building elaborate navigation structures (http://www.stim.com/ is a recent example); these often just get in the way, by increasing the number of steps it takes to get from "here" to "there."

Scott Rosenberg
Senior Editor, SALON
http://www.salon1999.com/

245

color clues

Even though I have a beautiful monitor with which I can view the web in millions of colors, I often put a good web site to the test by switching to 256 colors. If the site still looks reasonably pleasant at this bit–depth, I know that the designer has been responsible in making the site accessible to the vast majority of web surfers.

Margaret Gould Stewart
Creative Director, Tripod Inc.
http://www.tripod.com/

image information

One of my biggest peeves are when designers neglect to use the ALT tag in defining their images. The ALT tag allows those with Image Loading turned off to know what kind of image it is, and whether it is worth their time to load. Truly inspired designers even put the size of the image (20K, 30K, etc.) in the ALT tag. Those who leave it out entirely are forgetting that not all web surfers choose to load graphics automatically.

Gary Almes
President, Words In Progress
http://www.wordsinprogress.com/

Not all web surfers choose to load graphics automatically.

keep goals in site

There seems to be a shortage of designers that consider the entire user market during the page creation process. For example, web pages that use frames rarely account for frames–incapable browsers. If I'm using such a browser, I should still be able to view the page's information, just in a non–frames version. A business web page that doesn't account for frames–incapable browsers loses a large piece of the browsing market.

Jim Dierwechter
SW Engineer
jimdier@source.asset.com

All too often, designers design for themselves, or for the medium. Some sites are an abomination when considered from the perspective of user design. For some, it takes about four or five clicks, through graphics–heavy pages, in order to get to anything interesting. In other sites, you're presented with a screen in which you have no idea what to do. Mad clicking (what the Miller brothers—creators of MYST—call "thrashing") is not a desirable response from the user.

Do NOT get cutesy with your sites. Make sure the users can get to what would interest them quickly and easily. Why create obstacles?

> All too often, designers design for themselves.

Peter Merholz
Studio Archetype
http://www.studioarchetype.com/

I don't like gigantor pages with no point. Two months ago, having a Shockwave file on your page was kind of social order kind of thing. Like having a BMW, instead of the usual Mazda. So, people who weren't Director gurus chugged through the program and made these huge, over 1MB files that had a bouncing ball, and maybe some random sounds. They had no purpose, and didn't enhance the page. Even on a T1, it's a gigantic waste of time. Developers should have a point to their pages (even if the point is to be pointless) and only use the tools and technologies they actually need.

Jack Lyon
Senior Editor
PC/Computing

CHAPTER 16

PET PEEVES

247

html leftovers

I dislike incomplete HTML tags. You get to a nice page, and all of a sudden you see a /B> which tells you the designer forgot to check their tags, not to mention making you wonder if they bothered to look at the page.

```
Ewan Grantham
consultant
http://www.cris.com/~egranthm/
```

monitor madness

My own personal pet peeve: design for 640 by 480. There are lots of high-end, high-tech users out there, but according to surveys, MOST people browse the web using 640 by 480, and if your frames are designed for 1024 by 768 (or higher) resolution, the rest of the world either can't read them, or has to use slide bars just to figure out what the topic of the page is. It's *very* annoying.

```
Rebecca Allbritton
4th Coast Computer Services
http://www.4thcoast.com
```

image map insanity

In general, I despise image maps, because they don't give the user feedback about the URL they are about to choose. To me, the link information at the bottom of the window (that's where it is on the Mac version of Netscape), is an invaluable part of web navigation. It makes me very angry when people use that space for stupid, hard to read scrolling text (Javacrap), or when they use an animation whose update information similarly hogs that space.

```
Tricia
art director
http://www.cyborganic.com
```

My pet peeve is web designers who seem so paranoid about their site appearing *exactly* the way that they designed it that they make the whole page one big image map. I don't have the patience to wait for something huge to load, and I don't think many people do.

```
Willa Cline
http://www.willa.com/
```

original (valuable) content, please

Here's my peeve: web sites that are nothing more than the local phone book or yellow pages. If I only want to know that Joe's Autobody is at 136 Main Street, I can find it in the phone book. What I want from a web site is when Joe's Autobody is open, what they can (and cannot) do for my car, will they give me a loaner while mine is being worked on, how long to expect a paint job to take, how to fix minor body work myself, and so on. CONTENT, please!

```
Elizabeth C. Miller
Internet Marketing & Web Design
maxm consulting
http://www.oneweb.com/maxm/
```

A peeve: large corporations and successful publications that spend a lot of time and money repurposing content without adding anything truly interactive or useful or enriching, and without making the most of search engines, other technologies, or even their own vast archives. I think these sites are great at promoting traditional newspapers and magazines, which seem both a $ bargain and very interactive (at least you can read them whenever, wherever you want) in comparison. (While I do applaud them

249

for recognizing the importance of the web and increasing the amount of content available, I just hope they get more awake and interactive out there.)

```
Wendy Dubit
CD-MOM - The Family Place in CyberSpace
```

go back to school

Grammar rules seem to float out the window when web sites are designed. A particular personal peeve is establishing possession. Apostrophes land in places where they don't belong and are left out of others. Webmasters should remember that the web is a mode of publication and treat it as such. Unfortunately, we don't have web site copy editors; instead, webmasters need to take greater responsibility for creating correct grammar on the pages they design.

```
Erika Miles
Center for Health Care Strategies
http://www.chcs.org
```

privacy and passwords

A major pet peeve of mine is complex site registrations that can take upwards of 15 minutes.... all BEFORE you even get to know what you're signing up for (although these sites know a good bit about you before you've seen their first glimmer of content).

```
Wendy Dubit
CD-MOM - The Family Place in CyberSpace
http://www.cd-mom.com/
```

money for nothing

I am bothered by a changing link policy among more commercialized sites, wherein they are increasingly stingy—either selling links to advertisers or adding them, but in non-hypertext form. Understandably, they want to keep visitors at home (i.e., their home pages), but I believe this runs counter to the culture thus far built by the web, and I think that frames provide a pretty good solution to this anyhow.

I am always struck by the fact that, though many of the publication-based sites are very well-funded, those $ do not necessarily = passion, inter-activity, purpose, and pleasure. Indeed, I find more of those attributes among many of the underfunded but heartfelt entrepreneurial ventures that inspire me to visit the web again and again.

```
Wendy Dubit
CD-MOM - The Family Place in CyberSpace
http://www.cd-mom.com/
```

congruence counts

My pet peeves? How about uniformity? Simple concept, but hardly followed. The worst is when all of your pages are supposed to look alike, but they are all different widths, some of which don't even fit on the monitor! How annoying is it to have to scroll right, scroll back to the left, then scroll down to read a story?

```
P. C. Guagenti
Producer
http://www.guagenti.com/
```

fix it!

Pet peeve: lists of URLs that are not regularly checked for broken links.

```
Mark Loundy
Southern California Telecommunications Chair, NPPA
http://sunsite.unc.edu/nppa/
```

---

text advocacy

As someone who primarily browses the web in text–only mode (using Lynx on my shell account), my Pet Web Peeve is designers who omit text-based navigation, on the assumption that we're all of course loading those graphics. I'm not opposed to the graphic–'enhanced' stuff... but it would only take a few seconds per item for designers to include an ALT="short descriptive text" item in their web text. Without that, I see lots of pages that look like this:

[ISMAP][LINK][LINK]

[IMAGE]

[LINK] [LINK] with thanks to [LINK]

[ISMAP][IMAGE][LINK]

etc. Real unhelpful! I'm one of the "Dehanced for Lynx" team; see our info at <http://world.std.com/~adamg/dehanced.html>.

```
Daniel Dern
author, The Internet Guide for New Users (McGraw-Hill)
http://www.dern.com
```

most passionate peever 1...

I [bleep]ing hate it when designers aren't conscious of how their markup will appear in other browsers; for instance, <BLOCKQUOTE> tags as viewed in Netscape are plain text, but Internet Explorer italicizes them.

Ooh, I also hate it when people don't process their images properly and their GIFs are horribly dithered or their JPEGs are as spotty as a Clearasil-deprived teen.

"Coffee–pot cam," "Fishbowl–cam," "Toilet–cam," and the like are NOT viable substitutes for REAL content.

Yes! And little itty bitty pictogram–style icons at the bottom of the page that don't tell me ANYTHING and therefore are as useless as navigational tools.

Oo! Oo! Grr, argh, I hate more than one Black Box/Kai's Power Tools/etc. effect per page. If I see one more page full of neon/chrome/glowing/drop-shadowed type and beveled buttons, I'm a-gonna PUKE!

And yes, you may quote me.

Jodi Naas

253

most passionate peever 2...

Pages labeled "Under Construction." If it ain't ready for prime-time, keep it under wraps.

Same pages with the dinky little worker–dude–on–a–yellow–diamond logo. Does anybody else suspect he's actually shoveling manure?

"To see the rest of my site, click here." This reads awkwardly, breaks the flow of the text, and looks amateurish. Better to incorporate the hyperlink into the text—choose an active verb or evocative phrase that gives users a sense of where the link will take them.

Poorly designed forms. Simple things, like organizing questions into logical groups and aligning checkboxes, have a big impact on how likely people are to understand the form and use it.

Nonresizable frames—especially those that contain ad banners. If I can't make an ugly or uninteresting ad go away, I'm not going to come back to that page.

Missing noframes tag (or tags that say something like "Get Netscape 2.0 to view this frame!"). Not everybody can or wants to use frames.

Any reference to the web as "The Information Superhighway." These people oughta lose all their access privileges until they can prove that they aren't going to latch on to every silly, misguided metaphor they hear.

```
drue miller
curmudgeonly webmistress, vivid studios
http://www.vivid.com/
```

outside influences

guidelines for hiring independent web site designers

"Verbosity leads to unclear, inarticulate things."

— ex-Vice President Dan Quayle

Well, life isn't always perfect, and even with this and every other web design and HTML book at hand, you just may not feel like—or have the time—to create your own web site. Enter the independent web designer, consultant, or web design firm.

A look through Yahoo (http://www.yahoo.com/Business_and_Econ omy/Companies/Internet_Services/ Web_Presence_Providers/Web_Page _Designers/) yields hundreds upon hundreds of individuals and companies vying for your business. (By the way, if you plan on starting a web design company, I recommend that you name your company anything that starts with the letter "a" or you'll be lost among the throng.) Descriptions vary from "Why wait? You know you're going to have a web site sooner or later..." to "Creation and Hosting. LAN:WAN Internet Network Solutions, Turn-Key ISP Startup/Setup. WWW Marketing Strategies." And everything in between.

What's even more frightening than this daunting list is actually visiting some of the sites. A little side note: visiting "web designer" sites has been a major motivation in writing this book. It's unnerving to go to a web designer's site that has total disregard for even the most basic design principles, or graphics that take 10 minutes to load, or links that don't work, and so on. Major heebie geebies prevail.

I'm not trying to scare you, whether you're a potential client of a web designer, or a designer yourself. Just go at it with a serious "buyer beware" attitude, as you would hiring any professional. As with any hyped–up, new, hot, cool, in, gotta–have–it technology, people feel highly pressured to jump on the web–design bandwagon. There are lots of people who have learned a few HTML codes that now bill themselves as experts in the web-page creation field. A year ago, that may have been enough. Now we can be fussier.

OK, so how do I find a good designer?

Ask around! These days you can be standing in line in the grocery store and overhear conversations about web site design. The best reference is a happy client.

When you see sites you like, e-mail the webmaster and ask who designed the site. Many sites that are developed by outside firms also have a button or a link that takes you to the designer's site, where—hopefully—you'll be able to find a client list with which to further investigate its talents.

Smaller company sites or individual's sites that you like may yield a good designer. A cool personal site may be the work of someone with just the right talents for you to consider as a site designer and maintainer on a contractual basis.

💡 TIP: GET SOUPED

You know all those "cool site of the day" sites that inundate the web? Check them out, link to the sites, and see if there's a designer's link or resource. The best resource I've found for cool sites and web awards is Web Soup (http://lefey. cse.ucsc.edu/roth/WebSoup/). Claiming "No fancy graphics - DEFINITELY no GIF89 animations - No obscure imagemaps - No advertisements - No hit counters - No camouflage backgrounds - No buggy Java applets - No scrolling JavaScripts" - Web Soup gets right to the point of bringing its visitors a comprehensive and automatically updated collection of links from the oh-so-many cool/hot link sites that have grown so popular. This is a good starting point to find interesting and well designed sites to help you decide on elements for your own site, and you might be able to find a few designers to call on, as well.

Both the Interactive Telecommunications Program and the Minneapolis College of Art and Design host students' web work - a possible resource for a freelance web site designer.

Many major art and design schools now have classes in web site concept and design, and the students produce some amazing work. New York University's Tisch School of the Arts' Interactive Telecommunications Program students produce an online magazine, *ITP Review* (http://www. itp.tsoa.nyu.edu/ ~review/), which acts as both a forum for discussion and a showcase of students' web portfolios (or go to http://www.itp. tsoa.nyu.edu/). If you can make it through the Art Center College of Design's initial few pages (to understand what's on the pages, you need to reset your browsers font preferences and widen the page to a specific width), you'll find some amazing student sites (main page: http://www.artcenter. edu/). Another design school with some impressive student web work is the Minneapolis College of Art and Design (http://www.mcad.edu/). Check around in your local university and college art/design and computer departments.

what are you hiring them for?

Before you randomly start calling site designers for quotes, you've got to decide what it is that you want and expect them to do for you. Each level of involvement of the person or firm you're hiring may affect the amount of time and money invested in the project.

Here are some major elements of your web site you wish to have done by an outside designer.

I'd like the person/firm I hire...

- to plan the site
- to design the site
- to create the artwork only
- to create a company image
- to create web page templates for my company to "fill in"
- to create editorial content (text) for the site
- to maintain the site
- to maintain parts of the site, but I want access to the site's files for editing
- to interact with my site's visitors (i.e. to answer e-mail, take an process orders)
- to create a "simple" site (no special programming necessary)
- to create a site with lots of special effects
- to work on-site
- to host your site on their server
- to register a unique domain name for my site (i.e. http://www.your company.com)
- to train you or someone in your company to create and maintain pages

Make sure if you expect something from the person or firm you're hiring, that they actually know how to do it. Don't assume that they can do it all; all you have to do is ask them about their capabilities.

If they say they can do all you want them to do, ask for URLs to sites that they've developed and/or maintained that show off similar features. Ask for references from previous clients, if they are available.

For example, let's say you own a lumber company. If one of the services you want is for your site designer to create all the text content for the site, chances are that she won't have experience writing about grades of lumber, how to care for carpentry tools, or how to build a patio. But she may have resources for good writers that know how to work with you to create unique and well-written content.

clients from hell

How can you prevent becoming the infamous Client from Hell? I asked a number of designers to send me their wish lists—many of which stem from experience with clients that they felt just didn't have a clue.

First of all, become as familiar as possible with the web. If you've never been on the web before, or know very little about it, spend time browsing; do searches on Yahoo (http://www.yahoo.com/) for competitors' sites; click on all the navigational buttons on your browser's button bar to become familiar with their actions. Take notice of site structures that you find visually pleasing and navigationally intuitive.

```
Become as famil-
iar as possible
with the web. Do
searches through
Yahoo or other
search sites for
competitors'
sites to get a
feel for what's
out there.
```

260

Designers prefer clients to know what they want. If you haven't already, I suggest you actively work through my chapters on "Evaluating Your Audience" and "Brainstorming Your Site" so that you'll be able to provide your site designer with as much information about the goals of your site as possible. Are you trying to sell product? Are you looking for visitor feedback? If available, also give them details about your target audience that may influence the design of a site (do most of them use Macs? are they corporate clients with T1 access?). At the very least, the more you know about what you want, the less time you'll be charged for. Not to mention that your irritance factor drops tremendously.

Most of all, don't expect miracles from any designer or web site. Ignore consultants that harangue you to "put your business on the web and get rich!" Putting a web page up doesn't guarantee that you'll be famous immediately, or raking in a million bucks profit. If it did, I would be in Tahiti right now. On my private island.

Good designers also want clients who have realistic expectations of a web site and the technology behind it. This doesn't mean you need to know everything about Java and CGI and Shockwave and so on, but

it does mean that you should have an open mind about these technology's benefits and limitations. Don't go into a meeting with a designer demanding that "I want full-screen video on my web page!" simply because you read an article in the *Times* this morning that said it was nifty. If it's a technology that will hamper your site, or cost more money than it's worth (meaning, it does nothing to help get your message across), you'll have the designer rolling her eyes behind your back in no time.

261

what to ask for

Probably the first question on your mind is **how much will it cost?** I feel this is a question that should be saved until after other questions are asked, but let's get it out of the way for now. Pricing web site design, creation, and maintenance is the debacle of designers and clients alike, since this is a relatively new and rapidly growing field. The difference in price points range from about $100 per finished web page, to budgets of over half a million dollars (we're talking the likes of companies such as Time Warner). Some designers change by the hour, some by the project. All estimates should be at least somewhat flexible—since the web is a flexible, ever-changing medium, the stuff going on it and how it is presented may change (it probably has again since I started this paragraph).

How does the designer charge? Is there an overall flat fee, such as "$1,000 for 10 web pages?" Or do they charge by the hour? Often you may find that the costs may be a combination of the two. Make sure whoever you hire is clear on just how much you are willing to spend before she starts work. The last thing you need (I'm assuming) is a bill for 300 hours of work when you only have a budget for 100 hours.

Remember, **it's OK to ask for bids** from more than one designer.

Before you start laying out the cash, find out if the designer or firm will meet with you for a free **half-hour consultation or demonstration** of their previous work. (I can hear designers now... "a free half hour? are you kidding? I barely have time to sleep...") Many consultants, from lawyers to desktop publishers, have made this a common practice.

Ask for a client list (with URLs), or the URL to the area on their site that lists clients. You can request this before you meet with them; it's an easy enough document for them to e-mail to you.

You should probably be most interested in those **sites they've designed that may be in your market.** However, before you sign on the dotted line, find out if there is a possible conflict of interest. For example, if they are maintaining all of the product announcements for your site, as well as product announcements for their site, will there be a conflict of interest?

If your competitor is paying more, will they be a priority? I've never heard of this happening, but it's a consideration.

How will communication take place if the designer does not work on-site? While it's probably preferable for both parties to be close enough to one another to meet face to face at least once or twice, try to set up a plan for regular communication, whether by phone or e-mail.

Will you need to supply them with text and graphics? If so, determine the delivery process up front. Smaller files can be sent quite easily and quickly over most e-mail systems, or if you or the designer has an FTP site, it may be an easier exchange method. A specific folder for this web project will make it easier for both parties to see what has been sent and what needs to be sent. If a designer has multiple clients, files sent via e-mail may all end up in the same folder, which could wreak havoc.

If disks are to be sent back and forth, **decide on a delivery method**, and who will pay for the service. Since you're the client, it'll most likely be you.

Don't forget that if you are supplying text and graphics, **ask the designer what format the files should be in.** If you have the know-how and software to translate your huge TIFF images into GIFs, you'll save transmission time and the time it takes for your designer to translate them on the other end.

However, if the designer is going to be manipulating images in any way, she'll probably prefer to receive RGB images. Ask!

If the design firm is being hired to maintain and update the site, determine in your agreement **how often maintenance needs to occur.** For example, if you're publishing a weekly newsletter, obviously your site needs to be updated every week, and most likely, on the same day each week, by a particular time.

This is an important professional consideration, since your reputation for having timely information is at stake—if you promise viewers something at a certain time, they'll expect it. If it's late or missing, they may not come back too often.

If they are involved in the maintenance of your site, **discuss the mutual involvement of the process**, and find out the name of the person who will be in charge of maintaining your site. Discuss what your deadlines must be in order for them to make their deadlines. Agree on a review process, if there is to be

263

one. For example, if they are writing content, I'm assuming that you'll want to read it over before it's posted publicly on the web.

Hopefully, you're approaching your web site project with a realistic time frame. In whatever case, **discuss the amount of time and any specific deadlines** with the designer up front. Make sure that a designer has time for your project.

If nothing else, a designer may be able to **refer you to someone else** whose work is of the same caliber and same budget framework.

Ask about the designer's payment structure. Some may ask for a set amount up front; some may ask for the whole thing when the project is finished. Some designers break the project down into quarters or thirds; after estimating an overall price, the designer asks for a quarter or third up front, then subsequent payments on predetermined dates or milestones, such as after the site structure and storyboards have been agreed upon, when the prototype is ready for review, and upon the public launch date.

summary

If a designer encourages you to put all the hottest special effects on your site simply to show that someone somewhere creating your site knows how to make nifty-cool bells and whistles, chances are you're talking to the wrong person or firm. Remember that your site is meant to reach your goal, not to act as a site designer's portfolio piece. If supercool Shockwave is applicable to your message and suitable for your audience, go for it.

Before approaching any designer, work through at least the exercises in the chapters "Evaluating Your Audience" and "Brainstorming Your Site." The more prepared you are, the better off you'll be in the long run. You may just be surprised at how your site ideas develop, how much you know and don't know about your audience, and what your site's goals are. Just as you do research before you buy a car, research your own goals for a web site.

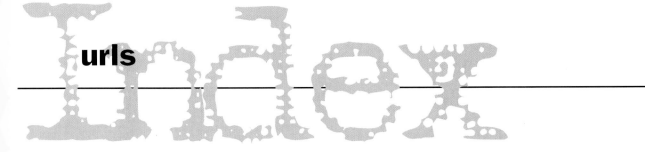

urls Index

INDEX

URLS

index

INDEX

269

INDEX

INDEX

INDEX

INDEX

277